Vietnam
Remembered Today

A Tale of Two Brothers

Vietnam
Remembered
Today

A Tale of Two Brothers

Vietnam Remembered Today provides a provocative look at two brothers who were in Vietnam at the same time yet their experiences were vastly different.

This Tale of Two Brothers unveils the personal challenges and circumstances of that time period.

Their stories represent what many of the 2.6 million that served in Vietnam endured, both in the rear and on the front lines.

This narrative provides the history of U.S. and Vietnam relations from the 1950s to the fall of Saigon in 1975.

Discover the battles and events that shaped the military and political strategies for fighting the war.

How misunderstandings by each side dictated reactions that were catastrophic for both sides in this conflict resulting in more than 58,000 Americans and 1.5million Vietnamese killed.

Publisher: Booklogix Publishing Services, Inc.
 Alpharetta, Georgia
 www.booklogix.com

Copy Editor: Sean Casey

First edition: May 2010
Second Edition: September 2010
Third Edition: December, 2010

Shaughnessy, Mark & Don
Available at: www.vietnamrememberedtoday.com
              www.Amazon.com
              www.unibook.com

1. United States Army, 101st Infantry Division
2. 43rd Signal Battalion
3. Vietnamese Conflict, 1945-1980
4. U.S. Army
5. American History

ISBN: 9780-9827399-1-4

Table of Contents

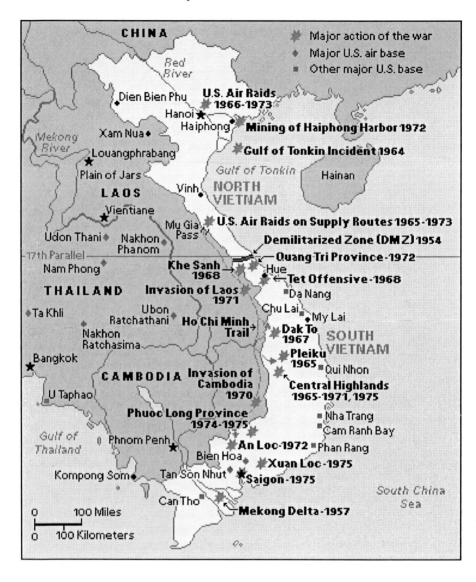

Vietnam Map

*Key Places and events

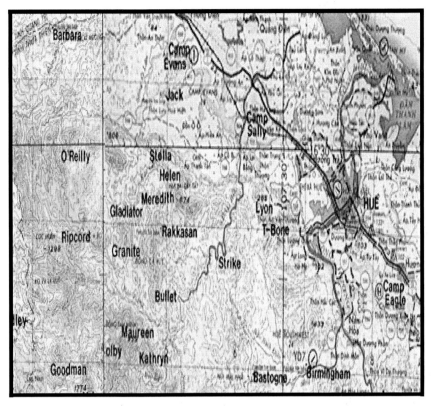

The Fire Support Bases (FSBs) shown were the AO, Area of Operations during Don's tour in Vietnam. Artillery was placed on firebases to support the ground troops and named for historical battles, units, and for children of the commanding officer.

Don traveled north through Hue, called the 'old city' and site of the longest battle during the Tet Offensive in 1968. He was first processed through Camp Evans before going to the field.

Rakkasan, was a large firebase that Don rotated through and it provided a shower and some relief but the enemy often attacked FSBs with mortars and sappers.

Don's unit Combat Assaulted FSB Maureen and landed on top of NVA and Sapper units that were firmly established. Ripcord was considered the last big battle between the U.S. and NVA forces, and we lost that battle.

Acknowledgments

We are grateful to all the people that we mention in this book as they had a positive influence on our lives. Our mother was our greatest influence as she was a wonderful role model.

Mark: We appreciate the friendship of those who supported us during our time in the military, and especially while in Vietnam. Jim and Jill Nyland encouraged me to complete the text from the outline and our initial conversations.

My wife Lisa provided input and completed the printing of the pictures, which was no small task. She said to stay after her to completion even though she had other things to do. To my wonderful daughters, Lannie and Lindsay, who love me unconditionally, especially after I slip them a twenty.

Special thanks go to my high school English teacher Mary Boyce who provided the stimulus for writing and research while completing projects.

We are especially appreciative of the copy editing completed by Sean Casey, Alpharetta, Georgia who provided the structure and punctuation that made us both realize that we didn't study our high school English nearly as much as we should have.

Ahmad Meradji of Booklogix Publishing provided guidance and structure for the layout, pictures and content.

Don: Thanks to my former wife Amy for encouraging me to write down my stories and to my daughter Katie, who is very supportive, compassionate and has a great sense of humor. I also want to thank my many friends who have been just that, friends. I appreciate a good laugh and we've had a lot.

I want to thank my brothers Jim and Pat, Sister Marge and their families. A special thanks to my brother Mark who nudged me and occasionally pushed me to do this writing.

Dedication

We especially dedicate this book to our mother Louise Shaughnessy who made us laugh at depressing times, and provided us inspiration and encouragement throughout our life.

Mark: A special dedication goes to David Ross, a Vietnam Helicopter pilot who flew men in and out of battle, risking his life for those he would never meet, and carried the scars of losing close friends in battle. He was a successful businessman, a great husband and father, and became a friend to Mark and Lisa and their daughter Lannie. To his wife Kris and daughter Allison, we love you.

Don: Thanks to Ed Deuschle, Edd Forrestor, Melvin Hollingsworth and John Fraser who kept me calm and alive during the hectic fire fights. I was honored to be around these heroes.

A special thanks to Greg Phillips (Greg received the Silver Star for his actions) for encouraging me to attend the memorial for Ken Kays, and for directing me to web sites and manuscripts for help with this book. At the reunion, I was able to meet up with more soldiers from D-1st/506th to include Ken David who received the Distinguished Service Cross and Steve Avgerinos a recipient of a Bronze Star with V for Valor.

Thank you to all the medevac helicopter pilots and crew who supported the grunts during firefights, and without their coordinated efforts and support, I wouldn't be alive today.

We applaud the efforts of the doctors and support groups at the VA who have been helpful as they continue to provide the needed services to many wounded veterans.

Back row l-r: Marge, Jim

Front row: Don, Mark, Pat

Don & Jim-First Communion & cigarette

Introduction

By Mark Shaughnessy

My brother Don and I were in Vietnam at the same time, yet our experiences were vastly different. We wrote this book to describe contrasting Vietnams. Don describes the life of the fighting soldier and I provide a glimpse of one "in the rear" supporting the fighting men. Until now, we only talked a few times about our Army and Vietnam experiences.

Don and I grew up five years apart in age, but close together in our likes, dislikes, music, and family relationships. We were active in sports and are loyal golfers. We enjoy Bob Dylan and remain great friends. I was twenty-four when drafted in 1968 and Don was nineteen when he was called into service a year later.

Vietnam Remembered Today provides a contrast of the challenges faced by those that served during those controversial times. The level of training varied dramatically, not only between us two, but among those that went into battle. I served with the 43rd Signal Battalion in the Central Highlands whereas Don spent his time with the 101st Airborne near Hue in the northern region.

Most of the servicemen in Vietnam never saw fighting action. However, more than 58,000 men died in Vietnam, and hundreds of thousands were injured, many very severely. More than 2.6 million served in Vietnam, making the death rate a little more than 2.2 percent, a price still too high based on the outcome of the war.

My Vietnam, from training to my service requirements, was less stressful than many soldiers. I spent eighteen months in Vietnam in a support function without any combat action. Not until the writing of this book did I realize the full impact of the war on Don, both in his training and his encounters with the enemy. He spent four months in Vietnam under enemy fire and, in some instances, friendly fire from other American units. His training was far more arduous. Under the duress, he built strong relationships with his comrades, some that remain to this day.

During some battles, the fighting was so intense that he found it difficult to remember all the details. In these cases, Don called on others who were there to fill in those gaps. Don and many of his fellow soldiers suffered injuries that will likely plague them for the remainder of their lives. Don saw buddies hurt and killed. He was involved in medevacing the wounded and preparing body bags for the fallen. His experience shows that war is ugly close up and reminds us of the sacrifice that many have made.

The Vietnam War was filled with contradictions. Those in leadership positions stated that our policy was one of limited action, whereby the United States would send supplies, weapons and munitions but the fighting would be done by the Vietnamese soldiers.

This "Vietnamization" program bolstered the idea that the Vietnamese handle the fighting; however, the number of troops and those Americans fighting in the jungles continued to increase. Although peace talks began with President Johnson and continued under President Nixon, the war continued, along with the deaths of more GIs.

Our story compares and contrasts what two men faced during the Vietnam War. However, the lessons learned may be shared among those in political power today. In the 1960's we supported an emerging, unstable government with little knowledge of our enemies' history and fight for independence while we were unsure of what we were fighting for.

After the Vietnam Conflict, many senior government officials from both sides met and compared notes. To their dismay, many key activities and strategies were totally misunderstood by each country, thus causing decisions to be made when not warranted and lives lost.

We believe this story represents many who served during that turbulent time in our nation's history and reflects what many soldiers endured during their military service and beyond. Our hope is to provide some perspective so others can better understand the challenges faced by those in Vietnam and other wars.

Vietnam History

The following Vietnam History provides a backdrop for the circumstances that preceded us going into the military. Vietnam was under French colonial rule for 100 years, who first intervened in 1861 and extended their control over Vietnam, Cambodia and Laos in 1893. Germany's control over France early in World War II led to the occupation of Indochina by the Japanese.

Ho Chi Minh was born Nguyen Tat Thanh in 1890. After schooling in Hue and recovering from illness in Russia, he was sent by Moscow to organize the Communist Vietnamese. In the 1930s, Ho Chi Minh ("the enlightener") organized a communist party called the Viet Minh that fought against the Japanese. After Japan surrendered in WWII in 1945, Ho Chi Minh declared Vietnam an independent nation, the Democratic Republic of Vietnam, citing the same words as the Declaration of Independence of the U.S. The French, with aid from the British, reclaimed Saigon and wanted to take back Vietnam.

Ho Chi Minh selected Vo Nguyen Giap as his key war time leader of the Viet Minh Army against the French. This former history professor was the architect for war strategies and developing the link for providing supplies, ammunition and weapons through what became known as the Ho Chi Minh Trail. The Franco-Vietnamese war lasted eight years from 1945-1954. During that time, Ho Chi Minh sent eight letters to President Truman requesting aid against the French.

The U.S. provided the French with weapons and financing mainly to stem the growth of communism, continuing our support for the French during World War II. Of course, it was France that provided the U.S. aid during the Revolutionary War against the British to establish our independence. The French were defeated at Dien Bien Phu located in northwest Vietnam on May 7, 1954 ending the Franco-Vietnamese War.

Because of international pressures on the heels of the Korean War, the United Nations interceded and negotiated a peace treaty that split Vietnam at the seventeenth parallel at what is called the Demilitarized Zone, or DMZ. Ho Chi Minh, the leader of the North agreed to the treaty only because elections were to be held in 1956 to unite the country.

Under the Eisenhower administration, Secretary of State John Foster Dulles did not support the Geneva Accords because he thought it gave too much power to the communists. Instead, the U.S. supported the creation of a regime in South Vietnam opposed to communism. In 1955, with the help of American military, political and economic aid, the South Vietnam government was formed.

The following year, Ngo Dinh Diem, a staunch anti-communist won an election and became president. Diem was harsh and oppressive against communists, jailing and killing many in the process. Moreover, Buddhist monks, nuns, students, business people, intellectuals and peasants opposed the corrupt rule of Diem.

The National Liberation Front (NLF) brought together communists and non-communists to oppose Diem, seeking to unify Vietnam. There is still a question as to how much influence Hanoi in the North had over the NLF. The coalition argued that they were a separate and autonomous organization. Washington discredited the NLF, calling them the "Viet Cong" (VC)) or Vietnamese Communists.

While some in the Kennedy administration strongly supported more military, technical and economic aid to help Diem and quiet the NLF, others opposed any involvement in Vietnam. Kennedy approached with guarded optimism. He increased the U.S. involvement with machinery and advisers in 1962, including Special Forces known as Green Beret troops to train Diem's soldiers. These 5,000 advisers were placed under MACV, the Military Assistance Command Vietnam. Soon, the NLF scored some victories against the South, and it was apparent that Diem's regime was near its end.

Diem's brother raided the Buddhists, claiming they were harboring communists. This move resulted in massive protests against the government, and the U.S. supported a coup against Diem by his own generals on November 1, 1963. Diem and his brother were captured and later shot to death.

President Kennedy was developing his own agenda for improving conditions within the United States. He called for tax cuts to energize the economy and he introduced legislation for improving education, public works programs and a civil rights bill. His domestic program was called "the New Frontier." He knew that he could not get involved in a war and gain support for his domestic program at the same time. Three weeks later in November 1963, Kennedy was killed.

There was concern in the U.S. that rapid deployment in support of the war would provoke China and/or the Soviet Union to intervene. China had its own internal problems as did the Soviet Union, but they combined to provide support for the war effort.

By 1964, there were 16,000 U.S. military advisers in Vietnam. Based on questionable attacks on U.S. war ships in the Gulf of Tonkin, President Johnson asked for more powers to wage a war. Congress overwhelmingly passed the Gulf of Tonkin Resolution in 1964 giving considerable powers to the president.

Johnson too had a domestic agenda that he wanted to accomplish that included many of the same issues that Kennedy had begun such as poverty, education, and expanding health care. In order to accomplish his "Great Society," he needed support from southern congressmen who would not support a president who was perceived as soft on communism. He was cautioned by his own advisers to solve this problem diplomatically, and was also warned by nations such as Great Britain, Canada and other countries to stay out of it. Even President DeGaulle of France who suffered a defeat after years of colononialism of Vietnam warned Johnson to stay out of Vietnam and to withdraw American troops.

Ironically, during the election in the fall of 1964, Barry Goldwater of Arizona, Johnson's opponent, was considered the "Hawk" and expected to lead us further into a war.

Johnson won overwhelmingly, with more than sixty percent of the vote, the largest victory by any president-elect up to that time. However, Johnson could not escape Vietnam and the number of advisers increased to 25,000 by the end of 1964.

Among U.S. citizens, there was early support for the war in 1965-66. Americans read that North Vietnamese Army (NVA) and Viet Cong were killing innocent villagers, women, children and old men while young men were conscripted into their Army. In fact, these killings totaled more than 60,000 during the years 1958-66. The Joint Chiefs of Staff wanted to expand the war quickly to support the new regime in South Vietnam. Others favored limited action, mostly bombings.

In early 1965, the city of Pleiku in the Central Highlands, played a pivotal role in escalating the expansion of our commitment to Vietnam. In February 1965 the enemy bombed the Pleiku airport, wounding 137 Americans, killing nine and 76 were evacuated. Less than a week later at Qui Nhon, located on the coast providing supplies to the Central Highlands, twenty-three Americans were killed and twenty-one were wounded.

Johnson wanted to negotiate a settlement through strength and he ordered a massive bombing called "Operation Rolling Thunder" in February 1965 designed to bring the North to the negotiating table. Using B-52 bombers called "Buffs", Big Ugly Fat Fellows, the U.S. bombed antiaircraft missile sites, bridges, supply and munitions depots including Laos and the Ho Chi Minh Trail.

In March 1965, U.S. Marines were sent to Da Nang in the northern region of South Vietnam believing that American involvement would require little commitment of human resources. The well entrenched North fighters put up heavy resistance.

President Johnson got caught up in the "war creep" and, in July 1965, an additional 125,000 troops were sent immediately to Vietnam. However, by the end of the year, the actual number was closer to 180,000. Bombing remained the main strategy and victory was considered months from becoming a reality. However, the NVA and Viet Cong kept fighting using jungle warfare tactics where they attacked and then retreated into the jungle.

The U.S. began using Agent Orange, a weed killer, and Napalm, a petroleum jelly, was dropped on suspected Viet Cong strongholds that also destroyed much of the plant life in the jungle. Unfortunately, these materials also destroyed the civilian farmland that was vital for rice and other crops.

The U.S. government increased the number of soldiers through the draft. Johnson was reluctant to use the National Guard because he didn't want to signal that the war was more important than it was. Also, Johnson wanted to implement his Great Society domestic plan, which was already creating conflict within the administration and the country.

There was concern in the region that if Vietnam was lost to the communists, other countries would fall like dominos; not only Laos, Cambodia, Thailand but also Japan, Korea, and even Australia and New Zealand. Some said that if the North Vietnamese were successful and we would be fighting the enemy on our shore lines. The communist Soviet Union controlled a large part of Europe after the Second World War. The erection of the Berlin Wall further exacerbated the situation. The communist Chinese were exerting its influence and there was fear that they would control the entire Pacific.

South Korea provided 60,000 troops, largely due to our support for them during the Korean War. Australia, New Zealand, Thailand, Philippines and Taiwan also sent troops on a much smaller scale. Britain, France, Canada and Italy were skeptical of our commitment, and strongly supported the diplomatic approach.

Although it appeared a contradiction that the U.S. didn't want heavy troop involvement in Vietnam, the government continued to draft troops and sent them to Southeast Asia in great numbers. In 1964, about 130,000 were drafted. But in each of the next three years, draftees exceeded 300,000.

The troops in Vietnam increased along with draftees. In 1966, another 200,000 troops were added to the existing 180,000 bringing the total to nearly 380,000 by year end. During 1967, there were more than 485,000 soldiers before the numbers topped off at nearly 540,000 in 1968 and into 1969.

In addition, there were approximately 30,000 troops in Thailand and Guam supporting B-52 bombers. Also, about 60,000 men were stationed on Navy ships in the waters offshore Vietnam providing air and artillery support. The number of soldiers would have been even higher had Johnson agreed to an additional troop request by the military.

On paper, America had superb weapons, pinpoint artillery, and highly trained soldiers. Plus, a vastly superior air capability with quick strike jets were supported by airplanes dropping bombs and napalm. Helicopters deposited and airlifted soldiers while providing supplies, fuel and ammunition.

The North had an effective supply route using the Ho Chi Minh Trail that ran down Laos and Cambodia bordering Vietnam. It provided the North Vietnamese Army (NVA) and Viet Cong (VC) armies with soldiers, weapons, ammunitions and supplies. This pipeline included a number of different roads and trails covering 1,000 miles from the north to the south. It worked effectively during the dry season and less so when the monsoons started. In spite of the challenges, the enemy used the trail extensively and it was critical to their survival.

The NVA and VC had experienced soldiers being conscripted until the war ended, fighting as cohesive units. They had the local knowledge and a vast tunnel system against an army unskilled in jungle warfare.

Their colonels and generals were in the military for life. The same leaders who fought the French were also in charge of the fight against America. General Giap held a high military position into his nineties. The North Vietnamese appeared willing to give up as many lives and pay any cost necessary to remain independent, as they had throughout their long history.

Although it was widely believed that their support of communism was their motivation for fighting, it was their fight for independence and sense of nationalism that sustained them.

Bombing of North Vietnam was often undertaken, but the Americans faced MiG airplanes provided by the Russians. Antiaircraft weapons and surface to air missiles (SAMs) were used in defending against U.S. aircraft. Some of the earliest prisoners of war were pilots shot down using these protective measures. U.S. helicopters and daring pilots were effective in rescuing many shot down using the Sikorsky HH-3 known as "The Jolly Green Giant" that flew out of Thailand.

Both sides were reluctant to expand the war but neither wanted to lose. The North moved from a guerrilla approach to a more long term war strategy, like they had just experienced with the French. Leaders from each nation felt that victory was just a few battles away.

Tet is the New Year on the Vietnamese and Chinese calendar. It is celebrated for fifteen days, commencing three days after the first full moon after January 20 of each year. This was a historical time for the Vietnamese to travel to their home and visit their family. In 1968, it was the time to launch an attack on the U.S. and ARVN (Army of Republic of South Vietnam) soldiers. Thus, Tet became a time of unrest among soldiers beginning in January 1968, which killed thousands.

General Giap thought carefully about the Tet offensive and began his planning during the prior summer. The North expected this strategic countrywide assault to bring South Vietnam to its knees militarily, figuring that many soldiers would be on holiday and the cities would not be on alert. They anticipated a popular uprising among the civilians that would favor the North, and expected to inflict a number of casualties while breaking the will of the United States.

Part of Giap's overall strategy to defeat the Americans was the "Siege of Khe Sanh," located in an area close to the Laotian border in the northern region of South Vietnam. Giap thought this was another Dien Bien Phu whereby he would surround the enemy, assault them and block supplies or replacements from being sent in to aid.

It was Giap's strategy to draw soldiers from major cities leaving the South open for the Tet offensive. Giap ordered 40,000 troops to strike at Khe Sanh on January 21, 1968. Unlike the French, the U.S. Marines and ARVN forces were well prepared when the attack began. Seismic detectors revealed that a large force was moving down trails through Laos toward Khe Sanh. Although there were only 6,000 American and ARVN troops, they had formidable weapons and firepower. The allied forces were prepared with helicopters, C-130 cargo planes, B-52 bombers, F-105 Thunderbirds and Crusader bombers. The NVA fought tough and the area wasn't secured until April. The Marines lost 199 in the battle but 9,000-13,000 NVA soldiers were killed.

The Tet offensive was a surprise attack that caught both the Americans and ARVN forces by surprise. The Viet Cong declared a truce for January 27 through February 3 to observe the holiday. In return, the U.S. and ARVN forces agreed to a 36 hour cease fire. President Thieu allowed most of his troops "leave" during the holiday with just a small force remaining to guard Saigon.

Unknown until later, the enemy had been stockpiling weapons for months, hiding them in tunnels, huts and buildings around the major cities, preparing for the uprising. The North attacked with 70,000 VC and NVA troops and expected the civilian population to rise up against the South and be liberated. Most of the major areas were attacked at once; five of the six major cities, and nearly all of the provincial and district capitals. Fortunately, one North division attacked a day early, on January 30, the original date for the assault. Apparently, they didn't get the memo to attack on January 31st. After the initial attack, U.S. and ARVN units were put on immediate alert.

In Saigon, protecting the Presidential Palace, the U.S. Embassy, the airport and the radio stations was critical. These were largely defended by local Vietnamese police and MPs that guarded these sanctuaries. Even those working in the embassies took shelter and were given rifles and pistols to hold off the insurgents. Although the enemy was high spirited, the execution of their plan was wanting, resulting in a poorly organized attack.

The North also attacked Da Nang, Hue, and Pleiku among other cities, but were met with Americans and ARVN forces on alert. Although the surprise attacks landed some blows, the allied troops withstood the surge. Tet was a military defeat for the NLF (VC) but a devastating blow to the U.S. campaign psychologically.

The Tet offensive inflicted damage to the psyche of those viewing the war back in the U.S. For the first time, television showed enemy troops entering the gates of Saigon, and Khe Sanh skirmishes were shown in America. When Walter Cronkite, the CBS news anchor, called the war into question, Johnson declared that when he lost Cronkite, he lost the American public.

The aftermath of Tet is still arguable as final figures vary. By February 3, reports show that between 35,000 and 50,000 communists died, while the Americans lost about 1,500 and the ARVN buried nearly 3,000. Some estimated that more than 10,000 civilians died and hundreds of thousands were left homeless.

In response to Tet, General Westmoreland, at the urging of the General Wheeler, Chairman of the Joint Chiefs of Staff, requested another 206,000 troops, with about 180,000 to be sent to Vietnam. These troops would consist of reservists that had some training and could contribute to the fighting force immediately. Johnson had resisted using reservists and asked for input from his senior advisors.

Johnson was frustrated at the lack of progress in the war in spite of his open comments to the contrary. In February 1968 Secretary of Defense Robert McNamara "resigned" to become head of the World Bank. Starting as a hard liner for the war, he became more of a "dove" as the war proceeded. He was replaced by Clark Clifford. Clark Clifford completed his assessment and soon began to realize that victory could not be assured, regardless of the number of troops.

Within a few months, General Westmoreland was promoted to the Joint Chiefs of Staff and replaced by General Creighton Abrams, who became commander in Vietnam. President Johnson relied more on his Secretary of State Dean Rusk who remained a "hawk" on the war.

General Abrams altered the strategy from search and destroy to protecting the civilian population. He implemented the Vietnamization plan and presided over the invasions into Cambodia and Laos. He left in 1972 to once again succeed Westmoreland as Army Chief of Staff. Abrams died in 1974.

Both sides agreed to negotiations in May 1968, but they stalled early over the shape of the negotiating table before finally agreeing on an oval one. There was considerable discussion as to who would be represented among the various parties involved. There were the North Vietnamese and the Viet Cong on one side and the Americans and South Vietnamese on the other. Of course, the North had the backing and support of the Chinese and Soviet Union. During the discussions, the South was adamant that the U.S. was simply trying to get out of Vietnam and didn't have their best interest in mind. This led to the Americans and North Vietnamese meeting separately to come to a settlement.

The North was unwilling to allow the South to remain an independent country, and Johnson declared that he wasn't going to be the first president to lose a war. Eugene McCarthy, a senator from Minnesota ran for president within the Democratic Party and his stance against the war was popularized in the New Hampshire primary, losing only by a couple hundred votes.

Soon after, Robert Kennedy also entered the presidential race and was gaining in popularity, stating that the U.S. should withdraw from Vietnam. Soon after, Robert Kennedy was killed on June 5th. Also, Martin Luther King was shot on April 4th, 1968, causing even more tension among the American public.

Backlash against the war continued and by now President Johnson's "Great Society" was derailed and protests began among the general public. In March 1968 Johnson announced he would not seek nor accept the nomination for another term as president.

It was during this period of time that Mark was drafted and began to see first hand what the military had to offer. This was a time of unrest for many in the country while some remained unaffected by it all.

Family Background

We grew up in the small town of Ashtabula, Ohio, tucked in Northeast Ohio on Interstate 90, less than twenty miles from the Pennsylvania border. Ashtabula has a population of about 22,000 that has remained virtually the same for the past fifty years.

Located in the Snow Belt between eastern Cleveland and Buffalo, N.Y., this small town's climate is dreaded by many yet beloved by others. Growing up eight blocks from Lake Erie, the winter months were fraught with snow and cold. Lake Erie would freeze over many winters from mid-December to March, impeding the shipping and railroad industries, and driving habits.

After the holiday season, people brought their Christmas trees out on the ice one hundred yards or so and a big bonfire ensued. Later, some thought that this ritual contributed to the dying Lake Erie, and the bonfires ended as steps were taken to restore the once clean and good fishing waters.

Winter's rain and cold winds slowly gave way to cool and wet springs. Summers were ideal with average temperatures in the mid-70s with cool evenings, perfect for sleeping, golf, tennis and boating. We rarely needed air conditioning, but muggy nights in July and August without any breeze required it. Some loved the "seasons" and would never consider moving, while others moved to Florida or North Carolina once their pension kicked in.

In the 1920s, Ashtabula was known as the Shanghai of the West as its per capita murder rate rivaled Shanghai, China. It was a port city that provided imported materials via railroads and ships. Coal from West Virginia was delivered to the Midwest and Canada, and iron ore from the upper Midwest was sent to the steel plants in Youngstown and Pittsburgh. Imported rubber for making tires in Akron ran through our town. At times, Southeast Asia was a source of rubber and some thought that protecting this resource was a reason for our involvement in Vietnam. Because of the high volume of shipments, West 5th Street was littered with a number of bars catering to the locals and shipmen.

It was a desirable location for businesses and families, especially in the 50s and 60s, but began to wane in later years as manufacturing located elsewhere. The economy has varied. Chemical plants once dominated the scene, but less so in recent years. Molded Fiber Glass, MFG remains a large employer in Ashtabula and other plants throughout the country.

Richard Morrison, a high school classmate and good friend of Mark has continued to expand the MFG business by making cabs for long haul truckers and now produces blades, cells and spinners for harnessing renewable wind energy.

MFG was the maker of the Corvette, and the Morrison's owned one of the earliest ones. We had an opportunity to ride in one of the first built, the 1953 model. This was a classic, although we didn't appreciate its significance for years.

Richard was a very bright guy and would have flourished in a private school, but his father was an ardent supporter of the public school system. Robert Morrison's foundation still fosters education by contributing to the nursing wing at the Ashtabula branch of Kent State University. Richard and Mark still meet occasionally and share a golf game and some fond memories.

The Cleveland Indians had some good years and many bad years with David Letterman quipping, "It's opening day for the baseball season and the Cleveland Indians have been mathematically eliminated from the playoffs."

The Cleveland Browns were competitive and we watched the great Jim Brown each week. In fact, Mark and good friend Jim Nyland attended the icy cold championship game in 1964 when the Browns beat the heavily favored Baltimore Colts. This event is well chronicled by Terry Pluto in his book, *When All The World Was Browns Town.*

Professional basketball was introduced later, and the Cavaliers first played in an auditorium in a rough part of town. Bill Fitch, their controversial coach said, "We were last in wins in the NBA but first in stolen hubcaps."

Ashtabula played a vital role in the Underground Railroad movement, moving slaves from the United States to Canada through a house that was adjacent to Harbor High School. Although Ashtabula was a small town, it produced many successful people including surgeons, physicians, dentists, lawyers, school superintendents, businessmen and a host of other people simply working in a field they love while raising a happy family.

There were a number of athletes awarded scholarships to prominent colleges and universities ranging from Hiram College, Ohio University, The Ohio State University and Notre Dame.

Denny Allan from St. John's played for Notre Dame and Mark Debevec, from Geneva, played for Ohio State. More recently, coaches have dominated the national scene. Urban Meyer, a product of St. John High School, coached the Florida Gators to a national football championship by beating Ohio State.

Our father Mark worked on the railroad and had an illness that required hospitalization. Combining travel with the railroad and hospital stays, we had little interaction with our father. On Good Friday, 1952, our dad died. Mark was eight and Don was three.

Louise, our mother, had to raise five children with virtually no income. She worked numerous jobs to support four sons and a daughter. Government assistance and Social Security benefits for children provided a nominal but important subsistence. She managed to put food on the table and we had better be on time or someone else would eat our portion.

The mid-1950s ushered in the rock and roll era. One night, we went to a friend's house and watched the first time Elvis was on television. At the end of his song, we all agreed that he should go back to Tennessee and hang it up. Boy, we were wrong. We enjoyed the music of the 1950s, listening to the Everly Brothers, Johnny Cash, Fats Domino, Ricky Nelson, Chuck Berry and the many other stars of that time.

We hung out at Lakeway's after school and met with a mixed group of people, much like "Happy Days." Back then, a shot of syrup was put in a glass and then seltzer water was added and stirred to make a Coke.

McDonalds opened in the last 1950s and was one of the top five stores in the country for a number of years. It was a favorite place for after football and basketball games, if the snow wasn't too deep.

After our mother won $1,000 in a church raffle, we were able to buy a television. We watched the golden era of television like the "Honeymooners," "Highway Patrol," "Burns and Allen," Bob Hope, Milton Berle, Red Skelton and Jack Benny. Our mother's favorite, Lawrence Welk, was on Saturday night and one of the highlights was in the fall when they unveiled the new cars for the upcoming year.

Mom took in laundry from others and was washing or ironing clothes continually. During the baseball season, she listened faithfully to the Cleveland Indians on an old white radio on top of the refrigerator while at the ironing board nightly.

In later years, she worked at MFG in a number of assembly line positions. Many people could not work with fiberglass, but if it bothered her, she didn't mention it. We tried to talk her into retiring, but she said she enjoyed what she was doing and her friends at work.

Once, she refused to send inferior parts to a customer stating that they didn't meet the specifications and they would only be sent back for the company to fix them. Bob Morrison got involved and settled the issue. I was proud that she stood up to her manager, trying to do the right thing.

This small town atmosphere provided little in preparing us for a world of war outside it, or so we thought. But, like others throughout the country, we were expected to meet the challenges and overcome them.

Part One

Mark Shaughnessy

Chapter One

Mark's Background

In my early years, during the summers, I pedaled my bike one block to the playground at Washington School. A high school student supervised while we played on the swings, and visited the school library. Since we could only play baseball if enough other kids showed up, I spent a lot of time reading. That library in the basement of the school offered my first real introduction to the world of books and I took advantage of it.

At Mother of Sorrows (MOS) grade school, I received my first communion, became an altar boy and played some sports. Throughout my football career there, my mother showed up for many of the games and I truly appreciated her effort to get to the games since she did not drive.

Early on, my brother Pat and I shared many household duties from washing and drying the dinner dishes, to cleaning the house. One of us cleaned the kitchen and bathroom and the other the living and dining rooms. Cleaning the living room allowed me to watch the Saturday football game of the week and the greats of Notre Dame, Georgia Tech, Alabama, USC and, of course, Michigan and Ohio State.

The summer of 1958 brought on a couple significant changes in my life. Dave Williams, a good friend from kindergarten through grade school, suggested I caddy at the Ashtabula Country Club (ACC), located about two miles from the Harbor area. Dave brought me out on caddies' day, Monday, when we could play for free until noon.

As a natural left hander, the only golf clubs I could get were in a barrel in the back of the pro shop, but they were right handed clubs. These were lost or discarded clubs from players so my set was a mismatch of odd clubs. I struggled to hit the ball right handed but had enough good shots to bring me back.

The second big change occurred when Dave came by my house and we went to Harbor High School to get his schedule for the coming school year. I was still on track to attend St. John High School but, for the hell of it, I got a schedule for classes. I went home that day and announced to my mother that I was going to Harbor as it was closer, about eight blocks, my close friends were going there and it didn't cost anything. She didn't argue.

Since we were Catholic, it was assumed that I was going to attend St. John High School about two miles from our home. My older brother Pat was already attending there, but he struggled to get to school by hitchhiking each day. There was no bus service, but there was tuition of a couple hundred dollars a year.

I was stunned and disappointed during mass one summer Sunday morning when a priest approached me and asked me to meet him at his house next door after the service. He and the head pastor strong armed me to change my mind and attend St. John's, telling me that my mother was going to Hell if I didn't go there.

Further, they said I wouldn't have to pay tuition, but I knew that my brother was told the same thing. He was billed at the end of each school year. I became even more determined to attend Harbor High.

Although Dave Williams introduced me to caddying, Dave Floor, another grade school friend, and I caddied virtually every day. Bill Hill, the assistant golf professional seemed to have us on speed dial, before it was invented. Often, we were ready to go to the beach when the phone would ring. We didn't have caller ID then, but we just knew it was Bill Hill. We caddied virtually every day of the week during the short summer to earn money for school clothes and for spending during the winter months.

High school passed with some disappointments. During my junior year we were heading for an undefeated football season. Early in the game against Madison, our punter dropped the ball in our end zone and they recovered for an easy score. In the final two minutes, one of our guys was called off sides three times in a row, stopping the clock each time. With twelve seconds left, they ran a play in my direction and I protected the outside. The runner faked outside and cut in leaving me flat footed. I didn't make the play and he scored the winning touchdown. Damn, not that I think about it anymore.

I was elected junior and senior class president. We met and discussed the objectives of our class. My classmates undertook a number of projects including car washes, bake sales and sweatshirt sales that brought in the needed funds. We raised money for the junior prom and left a gift to the school in our senior year.

In the spring of 1962, four of us went to Ft. Lauderdale. Our trip was inspired by the movie *Where the Boys Are*, that was popular then about spring break. Mike Kane, Peter Laird, Jim Nyland, and I drove to Florida via no interstate roads. Mike's father was kind enough and crazy enough to allow us to use his fairly new car. We all had a good time in Florida. I scored a hole in one playing one evening and had another about a month later in a high school golf match, but none since.

In my senior year, Jim Nyland and I went out to the country club in early spring to ask the pro Walter "Red" Lathrop for a job, and he hired us. I played on the golf team a couple days a week and worked in the pro shop other evenings and weekends. This began as a summer job but turned into a profession, off and on, for the next ten years.

I was asked to make a farewell speech at the high school graduation. Mary Boyce, our senior English teacher, helped me through it. She was an inspiration to me as I enjoyed her class and her support. I had little direction as to what I was going to do after high school. I had worked in MFG's fiber glass factory for a couple months after school in my senior year but knew I wanted to do more.

31

Libby Hall and I dated throughout high school and college. We visited her sister Mary Kay and husband Lou Masquelier in Cleveland and nearly crashed on the drive home. Mary Kay and Lou moved to Grand Rapids and we spent a Christmas there with her entire family.

My brother Don and I were strangers growing up due to the five-year difference in our ages. One incident brought us closer together. Libby often took Don to McDonalds since he loved french fries. When I was just out of high school and Don was a young teenager, Libby told me that Don really loved baseball and would like a baseball mitt for his upcoming birthday. I went to the up-town sports store and picked out a glove for him. From that time forward, Don and I developed a closer bond. I often shared my car with him and he let me use his motorcycle. Because of our age difference, we had separate friends but enjoyed each other's company.

In February 1963, I went to the west coast of Florida for the PGA School to prepare for a career in the golf business. I enjoyed the school, met a number of prominent players and golf writers and played the Dunedin Country Club, home of the PGA.

I stayed at Red's house a few weeks prior to and after the school. During my visit with Red and his wife Eunie, he taught me to catch mullet in his inlet behind his house. I caught three of them, Red filleted them and Eunie cooked them. We had a fresh catch lunch within 30 minutes. I also met Red's brother, Ted Peters, who co-owned and operated the famous Ted Peters Smoked Fish restaurant in Clearwater, Florida. He and his brother alternated months, each working only six months a year.

Upon my return from Florida, I was anxious to start working again at the country club using the knowledge I gained at the PGA school. In the summer of 1963, I roomed upstairs at the country club with the pro's son, George "Beaver" Lathrop. He introduced me to the music of Bob Dylan. Growing up in the 60s was special, with all types of music coming from one station. CKLW out of Detroit played music from the Beatles, Supremes, Stones, Doors, Temptations, Dylan, The Kinks, Four Tops and many others.

In the fall of 1963, my friend Jim Nyland encouraged me to give college a try. I was reluctant to enroll because my high school counselor, Bill Jones, told me while I was in high school that I wouldn't make it in college. He also warned me about being late in high school and said that if it happened again, he was going to send me home for three days. I smiled and said that is exactly what I was trying to do. I never really liked Bill Jones.

I signed up for three courses at the Ashtabula branch of Kent State, and studied hard. I did well in my first courses so I continued to attend in the evenings while working during the day.

Over the next five years, I lived at the country club with others including my brothers and the son of the manager. It was a good life with free food and an enjoyable place to work.

I worked at the country club in the summer and Carlisle's department store in the winter. Each fall, as the golf season ended, Tyler Carlisle offered me a position at their store for the winter. Tyler was one of three brothers who owned nine department stores in northeast Ohio. Two world events occurred that highlighted that era: John Kennedy was shot and the Beatles became popular.

When Libby went to college, she started dating others. Her friends considered Libby's dating as an opportunity for her to meet others and explore new venues. If I dated others, I was cheating. I said sarcastically that she reminded me of the Stephen Still's song, "If you can't be with the one you love, love the one you're with."

In the summer of 1967, Libby and I reconciled with a commitment to our future together, but she soon left for college and we experienced the same problem with her dating. It was time to move on. I didn't like how it ended, but I have fond memories of our being together, most of the time.

At least I didn't have to worry about a "Dear John" letter or worry about "Jody." Jody was the name for a guy who was fooling around with your girl back home. Regrettably, too many guys got letters from girl friends and wives who simply could not live on their own and either broke up with the guy or, worse, cheated on him while he was serving in the military.

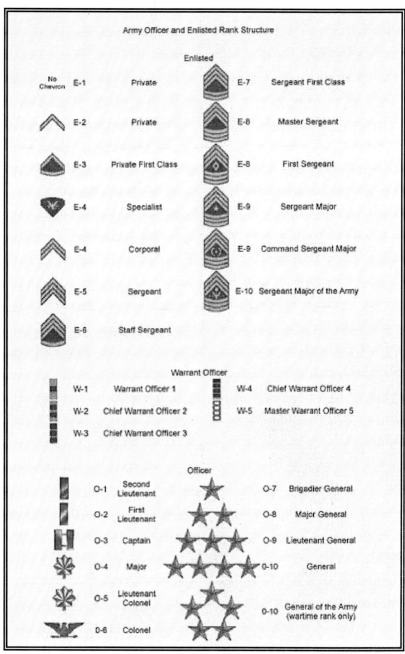

Army Officer and Enlisted Rank Structure

Enlisted

No Chevron	E-1	Private		E-7	Sergeant First Class
	E-2	Private		E-8	Master Sergeant
	E-3	Private First Class		E-8	First Sergeant
	E-4	Specialist		E-9	Sergeant Major
	E-4	Corporal		E-9	Command Sergeant Major
	E-5	Sergeant		E-10	Sergeant Major of the Army
	E-6	Staff Sergeant			

Warrant Officer

	W-1	Warrant Officer 1		W-4	Chief Warrant Officer 4
	W-2	Chief Warrant Officer 2		W-5	Master Warrant Officer 5
	W-3	Chief Warrant Officer 3			

Officer

	O-1	Second Lieutenant		O-7	Brigadier General
	O-2	First Lieutenant		O-8	Major General
	O-3	Captain		O-9	Lieutenant General
	O-4	Major		O-10	General
	O-5	Lieutenant Colonel		O-10	General of the Army (wartime rank only)
	O-6	Colonel			

Courtesy of Vetfriends.com

Chapter Two

Mark Drafted

On March 1, 1968, I received a letter from the draft board informing me that I had been selected by the Army to become part of the military service. I was at the bus station on March 13, at 6:20 a.m. to take a bus to Cleveland for a physical exam to see if I was fit for the service.

This was prior to the lottery, so virtually everyone was eligible for the draft with some exceptions. Those exempt included teachers, police officers, medical and dental school students and those married with children. Others got special exemptions through personal connections. I had been exempt as a full time college student, but it expired at age twenty-four. They figured that if you were still in undergraduate school at that age, you were only staying in school to avoid the draft. In my case, they were exactly correct.

I was taking a full load at Kent State at the Ashtabula branch. Once drafted, I was unable to finish my courses, so I took incompletes. I had little time to consider other options.

Some guys in Ashtabula that got drafted switched their major to education or went into the National Guard. I considered joining the Guard as my friend Dave Williams had done, but I didn't like the six-year commitment. It required six months of basic and advanced training, weekend meetings and a couple weeks of summer retreat each year. There was no guarantee of acceptance as the number of available slots was shrinking, if not closed.

I considered other branches of the military. The Marines were not an option. You had to be a little off to join them during the time when their life expectancy was exceeded by, well, everyone. The Navy was for four years and I wasn't crazy about water and being around a bunch of guys all the time. The Air Force had little appeal, having not flown yet.

The notice to get my physical recommended bringing enough clothes and toiletries for a day or so in case I was accepted. I thought of what might get me out of the Army but, with the exception of flat feet, I was in pretty good shape.

Along with a high school friend and basketball teammate Dick Huhta and Steve Grippi, a guy I knew from playing sports, and about thirty others, we met early that morning and headed for Cleveland, Ohio on a bus.

Steve Grippi volunteered for the Army. At that time, employers were reluctant to hire anyone that had not served in the military. In fact, military service was one of the first questions that would either qualify or disqualify one for a job.

My immediate future was uncertain. I paid attention to the war in Vietnam and knew that an increasing number of servicemen were dying, especially those in the infantry and their leaders.

I didn't understand how the military worked and what options were available. Much like parenthood and marriage, you just can't understand it without going through it. However, whatever was going to happen, I made a commitment to make the best of it.

As we arrived in Cleveland, we filled out paperwork, stripped down to our underwear and carried our papers with us as they checked our blood pressure and examined us for hemorrhoids and flat feet, among other tests. I took an eye test and passed, but later my ophthalmologist said I had needed glasses for years. The doctor asked me if my feet bothered me and I replied, yes, but as the day passed, I regretted making that remark. I had $33 to my name; I was tired of working during the day and going to college from 6:00 to 10:00 in the evenings. I still enjoyed working as the assistant golf professional at the ACC but knew that would come to an end.

Walt Perry, a friend from middle school, took thick files from his doctor and wore a conspicuous back brace to support his claim that he could not serve because of his back condition. Later that day, he was white as a ghost, not because the doctors verified his back problem, but because they found a heart murmur. He was sent home, and years later he experienced a heart problem.

At the end of the day, nearly all the guys passed the physical and were informed that we would be flying Purdue airlines to Ft. Knox, near Louisville, Kentucky that evening. It was my first flight.

The first stage of the military was orientation for three days that provided options within the Army. We filled out forms, including the beneficiary of a life insurance policy. Routine tasks of getting up early to make beds, eating breakfast and cleaning chores in the barracks accompanied the orientation process.

We got shots for every type of disease in the U.S., often getting them on both arms at the same time. Fortunately, I took them well while others flinched and their muscles tightened, leaving large red marks for weeks.

The Army provided uniforms, commonly called fatigues consisting of pants, shirts, shorts, socks and boots. Although I had flat feet, the hard leather boots were actually comfortable while walking and running in them virtually all day.

One day, a surprising one-third of the draftees were asked to fall out and go to a meeting. Later, one of the guys said it was for those who had not graduated from high school, and the Army offered resources for them to get their GED diploma.

During orientation, I was given the option of selecting my "job," or Military Occupational Specialty (MOS), in exchange for an additional year of service. I could have taken a chance of getting another MOS or infantry. OCS and NCO schools were offered, but those too would result in fighting in Vietnam. I wanted to pursue the best option to ensure I would return back home.

Another option included applying for Airborne, an elite group that parachuted into strategic locations, provided surveillance or encountered the enemy. One guy said that the training in the first week separated the men from the boys; the second week separated the men from the nuts; and the third week the nuts jumped.

After reviewing my history, I was approached about staying at Ft. Knox and becoming part of their golf team. We would play other bases and I could remain in Kentucky. Orville "Sarge" Moody, played golf in the service and he won the U.S. Open, both on the PGA Tour and the Champions Tour. I considered it, but declined.

Education played a role in determining where one might be slotted. If drafted with a college degree, the chance of going to Vietnam was about forty percent. A high school diploma increased ones chances to nearly sixty-five percent and higher for a high school drop out. Volunteers had a twenty percent likelihood of Vietnam. Because of the U.S. presence in Japan, Korea and Germany, about thirty percent of all soldiers served in Vietnam. President Bill Clinton and Vice President Dick Cheney would have likely served on a desk job and avoided the label of "draft dodger."

I elected to sign up for three years instead of two, in exchange for selecting "accounting," the Army's euphemism for supply. This was a fortuitous decision. Unknown to me at the time of my "re-upping," I selected the specialty that accelerated my promotion with no K-P duty, limited guard duty and more money.

The majority of soldiers were volunteers, although that statistic was misleading. A person eligible for induction as a draftee could "volunteer" and select a non-combat job. When I re-upped, I was officially discharged from the Army and reenlisted three days later and became RA, Regular Army. Technically, I "volunteered" for service effective 18 March 1968, the official dating system of the military. I told my mother that she was going to get discharge papers but she should ignore them. I wasn't coming home soon. Hopefully, avoiding infantry provided some peace of mind for my mother.

Basic Training

Regardless of what job one elected or was assigned to, everyone went through the same basic training. After three days of orientation, we moved to our basic training barracks, a two story building with double bunks a couple feet apart with foot lockers for each guy at the end of the bed that housed our clothing.

Being older, in good shape and six feet tall, I was selected as the platoon guide and Steve Grippi, Dick Huhta and Don Zehner from Ashland, Ohio were the squad leaders.

A squad is made of about ten soldiers usually led by a sergeant or staff sergeant. A platoon consists of two to four squads with a total of twenty to forty soldiers led by a lieutenant and a non-commissioned officer (NCO) as second in command. A company is made up of three to five platoons and can range from sixty to about 180 soldiers with a captain and a first sergeant as the NCO leading the troops.

Of course, in basic training, this was different as a Drill Instructor (DI) led each platoon and we acted as platoon and squad leaders. We were responsible for ensuring the troops were ready for drills while assisting in training and communicating relevant issues to the recruits. During the day, we worked on getting in shape that included running, push-ups and calisthenics.

We drilled on how to stand at attention, at ease and parade rest. We were trained how to salute, whom to salute and when to salute. You tuck your right thumb slightly under your right forefinger, parallel with your fingers and raise it so your forefinger touches the outside edge of the right eyebrow. We saluted officers but we didn't salute indoors unless reporting for a reason.

Overall, we were a mature, cooperative and supportive group of guys. We held sessions in the evening on how to prepare for inspections, and even how to properly fold underwear. Basic training was pretty much as shown in the movies with early morning rising, jogging, breakfast, drills, mail call, chow, and then off to bed.

One of the first mistakes was calling a sergeant "sir," as in "Yes sir." The common answer was, "Don't call me sir, I work for a living." The NCOs accused officers of not working hard.

The day we learned how to put on a gas mask was the day we were introduced to the gas chamber. We had false hopes we could use the mask that day, but no. We were told to breathe very lightly as we were walked slowly inside the chamber, hugging the walls so it took more time to get through it. They said if we tried to hold our breath, we would swallow greater amounts with severe consequences. I tried to hold my breath and then took small breaths when I knew I wouldn't make it through. My strategy didn't work. I swallowed a lot of tear gas in the last fifteen feet. When I finally got out, I just coughed and let my eyes wide open to tear up to wash away the gas. It was a memorable experience and it let us know that if there was gas in the area, we needed to get our mask on quickly.

The military taught new techniques using a numbers method. If something had four steps; it was taught in four distinct counts. "Ready One" and you took the first step. "Ready Two" and you went to the next position, and so on. It was a very effective process and the guys eventually learned the fundamentals.

There was a lot of "hurry up and wait" where we ran to our next station only to wait for twenty minutes for our next assignment. Even though I didn't smoke, I let the troops "smoke 'em if you got 'em" during breaks in training, sometimes to the dismay of the drill instructors.

We were taught how to use a rifle; how to take it apart and put it back together, in the dark, if necessary. The hardest part was getting to and especially from the firing range. We walked about two miles to the range and back to the barracks. At the range, we learned to aim and softly pull the trigger. The instructors cautioned us not to fire until told to, and stop when told to. Not everyone got the message and those got a slap on the head.

One could achieve marksman, sharpshooter, or expert being the highest. It was important to hit the targets. Too many misses, or bolos, was not acceptable.

If too few hit the required targets, the commanding officer got upset. Once, he decided that our penance would be to jog back to the barracks with our rifles held over our heads. Within a short distance, our shoulders ached, but we still had a long way to go. As the platoon guide, I ran outside the formation.

When one guy fell down from exhaustion, I stayed with him and put water on him from my canteen to cool him down until the truck picked him up. I then double-timed it to catch up with my unit.

As I got to my unit, another soldier nearly passed out and I once again provided water to prevent him from going into shock and waited for the truck to gather him up. I tried to catch up to my unit, but didn't make it as we were closer to the base. As I followed the other units into the camp, one of the other drill sergeants said for me to fall out with the others who couldn't keep up. I just looked at him and walked by to rejoin my unit.

The mess hall was standard throughout the Army. Everyone ate the same thing each day. Sometimes, the cook was allowed to substitute items, but if they were serving roast beef and mashed potatoes in Missouri, it was served throughout the world.

Some of the guys who needed to lose weight were put on restricted diets and ate at a special table. They weren't allowed certain foods such as potatoes, bread and dessert. Otherwise, they ate what we ate and lost weight during basic training. Although the food wasn't great, for some of the troops it was the best they had eaten in a long time. Over a couple weeks, the shallow jaws started to fill while the weak legs and arms began to tighten up.

About 5:00 each evening, we gathered for announcements and mail call. It seemed that some received mail every day and others never got any. I got one about every week from my mother, brothers or friends. This was the last act of the day prior to chow time and some relaxation. After a couple weeks, we were allowed visitors and had time to go to the PX for sodas, beer and snacks. We purchased books and magazines and got away from the barracks for a few hours.

Our Drill Instructors (DI), or more commonly called Drill Sergeants, were good guys. Sergeants Elliot and McCann were both young, about twenty-one. They signed up for OCS school, hoping they wouldn't make it, and they didn't. They had spent so much time trying to get in, it was too late for them to do much else, so they were assigned to become full time drill instructors.

Both DIs liked to party. On more than one occasion, I had to wake them up to ensure they made it for duty. The first time it happened, it was after taking our 6 a.m. run. We looked for the DI, and thought he was in the mess hall. We were due to head out for drills in about fifteen minutes, so I pounded on Sergeant Elliot's door and got him out of bed. He appreciated my getting him up.

The other DI, Sergeant McCann, woke me up one night about 1 a.m. and asked if I had anything to eat. We were not allowed to have any food in the barracks but we could not resist hiding some snacks. He said that he knew I had something and he wouldn't say anything if I gave him some. I told him they were in the nap-sack at the top of my locker. I went back to sleep and never heard about it. He later said he often helped himself.

Drill Instructors were pretty much what you see on television, getting in someone's face, about the distance his billed cap would allow. Remarks to an overweight guy might be: "Did you spend your time indoors reading a lot of books?" Then, they turned away and smiled.

They inspected us daily to ensure our boots were spit shined using black polish, cotton balls and water. We used Brasso to clean our brass belt buckle. We spent a lot of our evenings working on our shoes and belt buckles to ensure they were properly shined.

Near the end of basic training, we went on an overnight bivouac where we pitched a tent and dug a trench around it so water would run away from it. We crawled under barbed wire while bullets and tracers were fired over our heads. They told us there were live bullets and previously one guy stood up and was shot. It probably wasn't true, but it got my attention.

One evening, I was asked to come to the guard desk where I was told that my former girlfriend's brother-in-law, Lou Masquelier, had died in an airplane crash in Texas, leaving his wife Mary Kay and three children. I was deeply saddened as he was one of the great guys I met in my life. Lou was a real gentleman and a mentor to me in more ways than he realized. (I read that Ken Venturi, the golfer and announcer, was scheduled on the same flight but made the cut and cancelled his flight.)

At the end of basic training, we had a proficiency test and if you didn't pass, you had to repeat basic. We extracted our gas mask from the pouch, threw grenades into a bunker, completed calisthenics and ran a mile in our boots.

Upon completion of the eight weeks, most of the guys were promoted one stripe to private two and received orders for their next assignment, or AIT. I was assigned to Ft. Lee, Va. to attend a quartermaster school, or supply. Conversely, Dick Huhta and Steve Grippi took their chances and wound up in infantry.

Although the focus at that time was on who was going to infantry, others received orders for training schools for motor pool, cooking, generators, artillery and a host of other "careers." The reality was that there were thousands of different occupations within the Army that had to be filled.

As I spent more time in the military, I saw first hand the number of different jobs required in order to manage and support the combat troops on the front lines and elsewhere. In many instances, the training and experience in the military led to full-time careers once the person left the service.

Since a lot of infantry training occurred in southern climates, and it was the heart of summer, those guys were in for hot conditions. I began to feel a little better about my decision to add a year of service to avoid the infantry. Although Virginia was not as hot as Louisiana where the infantry trained, it was still hotter than northeast Ohio.

I had not earned enough time in the service to warrant any leave so I went directly to my next assignment. I don't recall the travel but I made it safely and without any incidents.

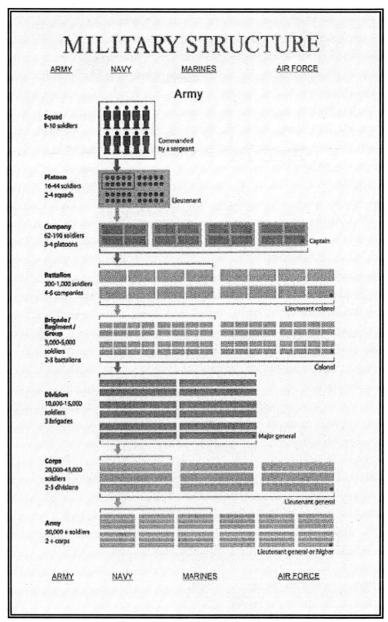

Courtesy of Vetfriends.com

Advanced Individual Training (AIT)

AIT was commonly mistaken for Advanced Infantry Training rather than Advanced Individual Training that defines your "job" in the Army. A MOS, or Military Occupational Specialty, defines a job in a combination of numbers and initials. Mine started as 76P20, then 76U20, and finally 76U40 with more training.

Once again, I was in charge of the men and responsible for keeping the barracks clean, the men on time and mail call. AIT typically lasted five weeks and our first session was from 6 p.m. to 2 a.m. because the number of attendees at quartermaster school exceeded the capacity of the day school.

I marched them out for daily roll call, using different formations to add some variety and to keep the guys sharp. We made our marching special and some of the guys chipped in and requested we do it differently. I invited some of the men to be guest marchers when they got tired of my same old marching orders. They discovered leading wasn't as easy as they thought.

Each day at roll call, I announced that all men were present and accounted for. One Monday, a couple guys took weekend leave but they had not returned on time for roll call. I was hesitant to pronounce them present, but I was assured that they were on their way. If they had not shown up or had an accident and not made it back, I would be in deep trouble. Thankfully, they showed up in time for class.

We learned from many different manuals how to account for the millions of supply items the military used. It taught us the procedure for submitting and tracking orders, and all aspects of ensuring the unit we supported had the proper amount of supplies. Since we had school at night, the hot days of July and August were often unbearable as the barracks didn't have air conditioning and there was little breeze. To get out of the heat, I often went to the movies during the day with another guy.

Each evening we marched from the barracks to the training room. Marching to and from class, we used other commands such as "column left or column right," and the group moved to the left or right. "Oblique left" had the men march to the left at a 45-degree angle, and the command "oblique right" straightened them out. This was effective when marching toward another group of men that we wanted to pass.

Once, as a pretty woman was approaching a stop sign in a car, I sent two guys ahead to stand in each lane to stop traffic, a common procedure. As we passed the woman, I commanded, "eyes right" and each soldier looked at the woman. She smiled. I was fortunate that she wasn't the wife of a colonel and busted me.

Another favorite was, "To the rear, march." This requires a clear audible command or some of the men keep walking ahead and some backward causing head long collisions. We tried and failed a few times, looking more like the Keystone Cops than a tight military group.

On the night of our graduation, a sergeant marched us to a building for the ceremony. Unfortunately, he didn't know where he was going and he started to walk past our building. I tapped him on the shoulder and then I commanded, "To the rear, march." The men did it perfectly and I was proud of the guys as they were.

We were given a challenge that if we won best barracks three times in a row, we would be awarded a Certificate of Achievement. Near the end of our training, I asked the lieutenant in charge when we would be awarded our certificates. He told me that nobody had done it before and he didn't even have any certificates. I said that I would get them and complete them for each guy and all he had to do was sign them. I got them and he signed them and the guys were gratified.

After completion and graduation from the five-week AIT on June 28, I was promoted to Specialist 4, or Spec 4, equivalent to a corporal. Our pay went from about $155 to nearly $210 a month. Many of us were selected to attend another advanced school at Ft. Lee in a different location on base. Others were assigned to Germany, Korea, or bases around the U.S. and Vietnam.

The new school was during the day and after each session, we were expected to come back and perform an exercise routine. We completed the requirement but with little enthusiasm. In the evenings, we reviewed the training manuals as we were tested once a week on the subject matter. The supply process was a good one when used properly, and some major corporations used it.

As the class president, each day I assigned a person to stay behind in the barracks to protect the property, clean the bathroom and polish the floor with a buffer from the supply area. After returning from class one day, I noticed that the buffer was still on the floor. It was supposed to be returned to the supply office at the end of each day. I reminded the guy on duty, a black guy who was about 6' 2" and in good shape, to return the buffer.

He said he wasn't going to do it. I was surprised at his comment as he was a very quiet guy. I approached him and asked him quietly to carry out his assignment. He again refused. Another black guy approached me and volunteered to return the buffer. I told him that it was this person's job and he should do it.

I told the guy that we were going to graduate in a couple weeks and get promoted another level with more pay and less duty. I was going to get the mail and if he didn't take it back by the appointed time, I was going to the sergeant on duty and tell him. The rest would be up to them as to what they wanted to do with him. I certainly didn't want to argue or physically confront the guy but I wanted him to know the consequences of his decision.

On returning from getting the mail the guy was on the top of the stairs with the buffer on his way to return it. Standing at the bottom of the stairs I said, "Well, here's your chance to drop that on me," and I smiled. Two weeks later, as we were packing up to leave, he came over to me and shook my hand and wished me well. I have always appreciated his gesture.

Upon completion of our second training course, we were promoted to Specialist E-5, equivalent to a sergeant and pay increased to more than $250 a month. In less than six months in the service, I was promoted to a level that normally takes at least two years.

The Army was in great need of supply specialists and they had a special promotional campaign that I was unaware of when I signed up. We were labeled "Shake n' Bake" or "90 Day-Wonders."

My brother Don and I were among those who completed Shake n' Bake programs and we learned a lot during our short but intense training. Although we were better prepared for our assignments, in reality, nobody was truly prepared for their assignments given the nature of the battle and level of responsibilities assumed in Vietnam.

The Army was known for being rigid but, earlier in our training, they asked us to elect some areas of the country or world that we would prefer being located. Although I didn't expect much, I put down the southwest part of the United States.

I thought this would be the only part of the country that I would never visit when I got out of the Army. (In the mid 1980s, I was transferred to Houston and a year later to Oklahoma City for two-and-a-half years.) So much for me knowing my future.

During my next assignment and through the fall of 1968 at Ft. Sill, the war in Vietnam continued with no end in sight. It was the important topic garnering attention during the election period.

As the number of troops and casualties increased, now referred to as "body count," Americans became more negative. The anti-war sentiment grew with a number of protests throughout the country and culminated with the riots at the 1968 Democratic National Convention.

Nixon patted his chest and claimed he had a secret plan to end the war with "peace and honor." He stated that he was going to "get America out of Vietnam." He won the election and became President of the United States.

Fort Sill, Oklahoma

After completing my formal training, I was assigned to Ft. Sill, Oklahoma as a supply sergeant for a signal battalion. I was surprised that the Army had granted my request for a southwest assignment. I flew into Lawton, Oklahoma on Frontier Airlines and, as I deplaned at midnight in late August, the air I was breathing was so hot that I thought I was going to faint. I wondered how the guys could play and practice football in that heat.

The next day, the company commander welcomed me. My job at Ft. Sill was in signal supply working at the base television station, providing transistors and other items when needed. We watched some television, including Paul Harvey, "Good Day," and otherwise worked as citizens do everyday, 8:00 to 5:00.

I met a couple soldiers in the barracks who became friends. One guy from Detroit was about my age, twenty-four, and we decided to take classes at the local college as we were bored just watching television in the evenings. I took Business Law and Adolescent Psychology, and these credits transferred toward my degree.

Another guy was much younger but had a unique talent to draw. He could look at a picture and put it on paper nearly identical to the original. I found it fascinating to watch him. One evening, he used a wallet size photo of Uncle Sam, We Want You, and copied it on to a large cardboard piece the size of a top of a dryer with minute detail.

Watching football was an excellent way to spend the weekends in the fall. Monday Night Football brought a capacity crowd into the recreation room, especially when the Dallas Cowboys were playing.

We got paid once a month in cash. We stood in front of the finance guy, saluted, gave our name, got our cash and signed a sheet stating we received it. Sometimes we went out for dinner to celebrate our pay day. Others played cards, and some lost their wages.

With little else to do, I saw a lot of movies. It was cheap--a movie, popcorn and a drink for less than a dollar. The library was nearby and provided music and books to fill up the idle time.

Once a month on Saturday mornings, we attended training sessions at the local movie theater on diseases we could contract and other related topics. One morning, the lieutenant in charge said, "Now, I want you all to get comfortable in your seats so when you fall asleep, you won't fall forward and hit your head on the seat back in front of you and I'll have to spend my afternoon filling out an accident report." He was my kind of guy.

Walking to work each day was enjoyable, but as the months passed by, the sunny day would be misleading. The cold air cut through my body and chilled me to the bone.

I called my mother from a pay phone each Sunday. My brother Pat was a few months shy of two years older than me, and he struggled emotionally in 1968. He had been dating a lady for some time and when she broke it off, he went into a tail spin. When I talked with my mother one Sunday, it was the only time I remember her crying from seeing her son struggle.

The February morning I received my orders for Vietnam, I was stunned. Although it was somewhat expected, it is still disheartening when it happens. My emotions ran from fear for myself, the impact it makes on the rest of the family, and fear of the unknown.

As I told my buddies that I was going off to the real war, my Detroit friend, in his sarcastic way said, "Well, I hate to see you go, but better you than me."

As I was preparing to take some leave in Ashtabula, I wanted to get from Ft. Sill, about forty miles south of Oklahoma City to Tulsa, about ninety miles north of OKC. The usual options were to take a flight or a taxi but both cost a lot of money. I was talking to some guys and one lifer sergeant suggested I hitch a ride on a flight from the Air Force base. He put me in touch with a guy, and he told me when and where to show up. When I arrived, I asked the captain the purpose of his flight and he said, "You are."

I felt pretty good about that. As we took off in this four-seat modest plane with me in the co-pilot seat with a helmet and head phones on, he explained that he needed to fly so many hours each month to maintain his license, so he was happy to take me. He showed me the instrument panel and how he dialed into a Tulsa radio station to guide us and then use his telephone with the local tower to bring us into the final flight plan. Cool experience. I then flew into Cleveland and then took a train to Ashtabula, an excellent way to travel. While at home, I visited my friends and family and reminded my mother that I had a safe assignment and she shouldn't worry. I would do all the worrying for the both of us.

The Army pays a per mile rate for travel so, in an attempt to save some money, I hitched rides with the Air Force whenever possible rather than pay for a commercial flight. I pocketed the difference between what they paid me and the cost. My trip to Vietnam started with an Air Force flight to San Bernardino, California then to San Francisco where I spent a night at the Presidio, a military base. The next day I took a bus tour of San Francisco and then later a flight to Ft. Lewis, Washington.

During the orientation process, we got our orders, shots for malaria and other infectious diseases and clothing better suited for the Vietnam climate. Boots were made from a light mesh material supported by leather uppers, and a thin but hard steel plate was inserted in the rubber bottoms to prevent injury when walking through the jungle. The enemy created booby traps, notably punji sticks, a sharp bamboo piece coated with feces, to inflict severe injury or death. The boots had small holes along the bottom sides for drainage during the monsoon season.

I received jungle fatigues, clothing made from light weight material that was cooler for the hotter temperatures and dried quickly after a rain. It had a mosquito repellent built into the material although many in the field questioned its effectiveness.

I was apprehensive about my tour in Vietnam. I heard stories of guys who worked in their specialty but also had to pick up their weapons regularly and fight the enemy to protect their area of operations. Either way, I was getting mentally prepared for it.

43rd Signal Battalion HQ

Screens, Supply Bldg-Right

Chapter Three

Vietnam-Mark

I was in country only four days when a rocket came in about six a.m. and exploded in the middle of the compound, throwing shrapnel in all directions. It was the dry months so dust flew for a couple hundred feet. I was knocked out of my bunk. I slipped into my fatigues and boots, grabbed my weapon and helmet, and made my way rapidly to the bunker next to my quarters. I sat there in the early morning convinced that I would not make it through my tour.

As I was flying over the Pacific Ocean toward Vietnam in March 1969, I reminded myself that 98 percent of all soldiers that went there came back. Of those that did not make it, many were 11 Bravo infantry, or those who commanded them. I wasn't either.

The trip to Vietnam is a long one. Surprisingly, the flights to Vietnam were on commercial airlines like American Airlines and we were treated like other commercial flyers. As we entered into new time zones over the Pacific, we were stuck at dinnertime, eating steak every meal during each of the roughly four hour flights between San Francisco to Hawaii to Guam to the Philippines and on to Saigon. The stops in each location were uneventful. They were relatively short, lasting from thirty minutes to an hour for refueling. Waiting outside the Hawaii airport on the way to an uncertain future is not paradise.

As we were landing at Ton Son Nhut airport in Saigon, Vietnam, I was expecting to be fired upon from snipers hiding in the jungle. I walked from the airplane, down the airplane steps and across the tarmac to a waiting bus without incident.

There were four major tactical zones in Vietnam called Corps. Each Corps had to be properly supported and managed. The logistics of providing tons of food, ammunition, and other items was a massive task requiring numerous ships and planes carrying these supplies. Each squad, platoon, company, battalion and brigade had to be fortified with these necessities, and without fail.

This was no small task. All of the food and other supplies had to be sent in, making the logistics of providing the required items a massive and expensive operation. It all seemed to make sense and the military had experience in these matters, but it is quite remarkable that they were able to pull it off, at least most of the time.

Air support for our troops on the ground was provided by different military units. The Army provided helicopters for delivering and extracting troops. The Air Force kept the North Vietnamese pilots and MiGs from going into South Vietnam and also provided the bombing of strategic locations. Navy ships in the Gulf of Tonkin and S. China Sea supported the ground troops with long range air and artillery support.

I (eye) Corps was in the northern region near the DMZ, or Da Nang, and both of these locations were known for widespread fighting activity. (Note: Spelling of Da Nang varies.) II Corps was located in the Central Highlands and, although many early battles were fought there, the fighting eased up during my time in-country. III Corps was located around Saigon in the southern region of the country. IV Corps was in the southernmost part of South Vietnam.

March of 1969 was hot and dry. When I arrived, I had my orders for the 43rd Signal Company in Pleiku in the Central Highlands. Awaiting transportation, I was called and told to get on a plane designated for Da Nang. I was surprised and informed the guy that I had orders for Pleiku and he must be mistaken.

After a couple days, the guys in Personnel straightened it out and I received my original orders for Pleiku. I was ushered aboard a C-130, a unique airplane that is a slow, functional plane, loaded with heavy equipment, Vietnamese and GIs in transit.

It could land and take off on short runways to pick up people and deliver supplies to remote locations. Typically, the plane had no seats in the back so hanging on to the straps along the inside of the plane was the equivalent to fastening your seat belt. In some instances, the back of the plane was open so I held on a little tighter.

I arrived in Pleiku when the number of American soldiers in Vietnam was at the highest level with nearly 540,000 serving there. For every person in the field fighting, eight to ten were in support; motor pool, artillery, finance, cooks, transportation and supply among others. Those of us in the "rear echelon" had it nice compared to those in the bush.

Louis McDonough, a guy in our unit, met me at the airport. It had not rained for months and the dust quickly covered the top of my boots. The spit shine on boots demanded in the States was not expected in Nam. I threw my duffel bag in the back seat of the jeep and viewed the countryside nervously as he drove the mile between the Pleiku airport and the base camp. The Air Force base was on the right for a half-mile until we turned right and drove another half-mile up a small incline past the medical base camp. We entered through the gates to the 43rd Signal Battalion that was to be my home for the next eighteen months.

Vietnam was located on about the same latitude as Central America but, without the trade winds, it was hot and humid. In Saigon and Da Nang, daily temperatures averaged about ninety degrees. Plus, it was humid from the rivers that flowed through the Mekong Delta near Saigon.

The temperatures in Pleiku in the Central Highlands were milder since the area was elevated above sea level. It was still very warm most of the year with temperatures dropping only in December and January.

The rainy monsoons included afternoon thunderstorms to all-day downpours and the Vietnam monsoon season varied by region. Near Da Nang, in the northern region, the monsoon ranged from April to October with the dry season from November to March. It was hot year round, but especially in June, July and August.

Near Saigon and the Mekong Delta, the heavy rains came between May and November but it remained muggy and warm to hot year–around, with average temperatures ranging from 84 to 92 degrees. The dry season was from December through April, providing little relief from the stifling hot and steamy conditions.

The monsoon season was different for the Central Highlands. There, it rained from August to December, cooled for a couple months and then the dry season lasted from January through July.

It was important to recognize the regional differences because the rains impacted field operations. During the rainy season, poor visibility and muddy ground impeded supply of vital equipment. American helicopter activity was curtailed by poor weather. The low visibility resulted in more accidents, slower flying and higher maintenance. There was less fighting during the monsoon season, providing time for troops to regroup for the dry season.

Low visibility hindered sapper attacks as well. Sappers were a select group of the enemy that set ambushes and would sneak up on our troops with grenades, AK-47 rifles and explosive charges. They crawled through mine fields and barbed wire to blow up bases, airfields and ships anchored in South Vietnam harbors.

Pleiku was located about twenty-five miles from the Cambodian border and was no stranger to some fierce battles. Had I known this history at the time, perhaps I would have been less anxious to insist on Pleiku as my final destination.

The battle in the Ia Drang Valley, just south of Pleiku was one of the earliest engagements between the North Vietnamese and Americans. In November 1965, the U.S. knew that some VC and perhaps the NVA were located in that region and sent the 7th Cavalry to "search and destroy" as many of the enemy as possible. This encounter was a test of strength, wills and strategies for both sides.

The Americans were using the Bell UH-1 (Huey) helicopters to deliver troops and later extract them from the area. The Huey helicopters had many versions designed for specific reasons. The UH-1 was the expanded version that held 10-12 soldiers and was loaded with an M-60 machine gun and gunner.

The troop transport models, the UH-1D, were called Slicks as they didn't have any bells and whistles. There were other versions used for medevac, command centers and slings for medium weight combat loads. The gun ships traveling at a speed of about 110 knots carried rockets, 20mm cannons and M60 machine guns.

Lieutenant Colonel Harold Moore, a 1945 graduate of West Point and veteran of the Korean War led the troops, being the first one to land and the last one to leave. The Hueys traveled in four groups of four depositing the troops on Landing Zone (LZ) X-Ray, about the size of a football field.

The enemy of nearly 2,000 VC soldiers was led by General Man. His strategy was to determine how to fight the Americans and this was his first test. Although LZ X-Ray appeared to be just an open field, it was surrounded by heavy jungle and a mountain region. The enemy forces were prepared to battle the initial 430-450 men of the 1st Battalion, 7th Cavalry. When the Americans landed and spread out, they were met with mortar rounds, sniper and machine gun fire.

Lt. Colonel (later General) Harold Moore called in air and artillery support. Gun ships were limited to where they could fire to avoid hitting their own soldiers who were fighting along the perimeter. Chinook helicopters lifted twelve artillery guns to a nearby LZ, where they began to hammer the enemy. Moore stated that the artillery and air strikes turned the tide and they left with 79 soldiers dead and another 120 wounded, far less that the enemy with 643 dead. It was difficult to get an accurate body count of the enemy as they and the Americans were diligent about taking their dead and wounded with them whenever possible. General Man also learned his lesson and never again took such risks with a large number of troops against the American's superior firepower.

The strategic maneuvers of transporting troops via helicopters supported by gun ships while landing and backed by artillery fire and air strikes was the prescription for fighting for the rest of the war. This battle is described in detail in *We Were Soldiers and Young* by Moore & Galloway, and *The Soldiers' Story* by Ron Steinman.

The Central Highlands was the home of a large communications network. The 43rd Signal Battalion was activated in October 1966 in Pleiku as a combat support battalion communications center, supporting both US and ARVN forces in the II Corps Tactical Zone. We had screens over 150 feet high and sixty feet wide sending messages throughout the country.

I was in battalion headquarters that not only supported our Pleiku operation that included MACV, but also our outlying companies in Kontum, An Khe, and Ban Me Thout. Kontum was located about fifty miles north of Pleiku. An Khe was a similar distance east and Ban Me Thout was about ninety miles south of Pleiku.

A battalion consists of four to six companies and about 300 to 1,000 soldiers commanded by a lieutenant colonel with a command sergeant major as the NCO assistant. In our case, and quite common, an Executive Officer (XO) major was the second in command. Our battalion reported to 1st Signal Brigade in Saigon and that included two to five battalions with about 3,000 to 5,000 soldiers led by a full colonel with a command sergeant major. I only had one encounter with anyone from brigade and it was a positive one.

Our primary task was providing telephone support for the 4th Infantry Division at Camp Enari. In early 1968, enemy activity culminated with the Tet offensive in January 1968. All 43rd Signal units were attacked and Company C in Kontum was nearly overrun. Those who were there did not forget the attack and those who followed knew about it.

In 1969, when I arrived, supporting the 4th Infantry Division remained the centerpiece of our mission. Our tasks shifted as bases were transferred to other units and technology improved.

There were about four sergeants, six corporals and several privates in our supply unit. Entering our office, I was in the far back left corner, and along the back wall were three other guys at their steel framed desks with filing cabinets along the wall.

To the immediate right was Sergeant First Class Wilson, a twenty plus-year lifer, who was in charge of the NCOs. Behind him was Chief Warrant Officer (CW2) Ives. There was an adjoining office next to my area that Lt. Queen filled.

After introductions to my coworkers, I was shown to my barracks where I unpacked. I shared a ten by twelve foot room with three other guys. The sergeant's quarters on the first floor had separate rooms large enough to fit four soldiers. There were two sets of bunk beds with enough room between for two people to stand. The second floor was open with some separate rooms for sergeants, or E-5s. There was electricity for lights, radios, refrigerators and stereo equipment supported by the generator shop.

The entrance to each room typically had long beads hanging from the top of the doorway. Privacy was a relative term and we expected interruptions. We stored our possessions in one of four wall lockers that were about six feet high, four feet wide and three feet deep. The inside of the lockers was designed to retrieve our items in the dark. Our helmet was on top, shoes at bottom left, shirts on the left and pants on the right with socks in the bottom drawer and underwear in the top one.

The weapon was inside left and ammunition was next to it. A flashlight was on the top left next to the playing cards. At one time, my locker had a M-60, a M-16 rifle and a .45 caliber pistol, but I never fired a shot except at the firing range. We preset the padlocks so it opened by simply moving it to the right a few numbers so we could open it quickly in the dark.

Although not everyone needed a mosquito net, I clearly did. I have always drawn mosquitoes, and they hunted me down like predators. Even if I had just a small hole in the net the size of a dime, I had to get up and put some tape over the hole.

The barracks were relatively new, built about a year before my arrival by some of the guys that were still there. Prior to the barracks, the soldiers lived in tents. The four barracks were two stories high, about ninety feet long and thirty feet wide.

They were lined up two and two on each side with a walkway between them leading to the showers. The barracks had a three foot mesh screen along the outside, about eye level, and a mesh screen window in each room to aid circulation and reduce the bugs-- especially the malaria carrying mosquitoes.

Surrounding the barracks were sand bags about five feet high for protection from mortars or rockets. We rarely got a serious threat of rockets because it was said that the North Vietnamese used the screens like we did to communicate with others.

I was in country only four days when a rocket came in about six a.m. and exploded in the middle of the compound throwing shrapnel in all directions. It was the dry months so dust flew for a couple hundred feet. I was knocked out of my bunk. I slipped into my fatigues and boots, grabbed my weapon and helmet, and made my way rapidly to the bunker next to my quarters. I sat there in the early morning convinced that I would not make it through my tour.

The sand bags were of little help to those on the second floor. When the rocket landed, shrapnel went through the wood siding about 30 feet away, through a locker and lodged about four inches into a two- by-six piece of wood. A guy in his bunk, inches away from the flying shrapnel, was not touched. If we raised the sand bags higher, the air flow would be stifled and guys would cook to death. The goal was to get a downstairs room, and I had one.

A soldier on his final day in country heading home was not so lucky. He changed his habit of not eating breakfast. He thought he needed some food since he would be busy with a flight to Saigon, and getting processed to go home. As he was walking back from the mess hall, the rocket landed about twenty feet in front of him and the blast spun him around. He got hit in the right butt cheek.

His final words to everyone as he was taken away were, "Don't ever change your habits." He went to the nearby hospital where he recovered for three days and then was sent home.

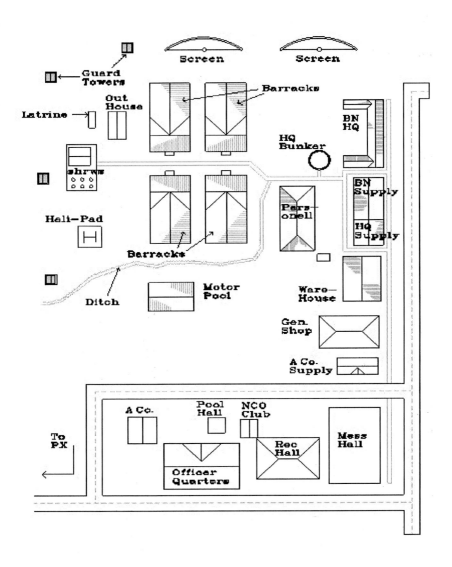

43rd Signal Battalion Compound

Courtesy of Rob Padgett

Toward the perimeter past the barracks, there was an outhouse on the right with eight seats with holes. Cans, about two feet in diameter, were placed a couple feet under the holes. A Vietnamese man changed the cans daily, pouring kerosene on the waste and burning it. Not bad as long as the wind was blowing in the right direction.

One time, I was sitting there talking with a guy about hometowns, sports and such when he jumped a little. He sat down and a few seconds later, he jumped up again and looked through the hole. The Vietnamese man was poking him on his butt and motioning for him to move over to the next hole. The GI told the man to get the hell out of there and sat back down. Urinals were pipes outside surrounded by lime, called piss-tubes. Not pretty and smelled terrible.

The shower was the final building before the perimeter. On the right side were a set of six showers separated by a brick wall with sinks on the left side. To get a hot shower, we had to get there by 7 a.m. or it was cold, especially in the winter. Even then, the walk from the showers to the barracks in just a towel was chilling and, yes, there was shrinkage.

When we had all night duty, we took a shower later in the morning when the water was warm. The Vietnamese laundry women occupied the same area so we took our shower in front of them. They pretended not to notice, and they didn't point or laugh at us.

The final important marker beyond the bunkers was the helipad, where the helicopters landed to pick up or drop off passengers and others who visited or left the battalion.

There were four bunkers that we manned when on alert. These were large enough to house four to six men with sand bags several feet wide and high to protect from enemy mortars. Beyond the towers and bunkers was a flat area where claymore mines, trip flares and concertina wire made entry almost impossible. We heard of the well-trained sappers' ability to get through just about anything, so we were always aware that someone could attack us.

The wood slat walkways were elevated to keep our feet out of the dust in the dry season and out of the mud during the monsoons. They were about four to six inches off the ground and about four feet wide, designed to ensure water could flow beneath. They linked the buildings with each other and the mess hall.

My job was to provide equipment and supplies ranging from underwear to two-and-a-half ton trucks. Upon arrival, I immediately took an inventory and found we had very few supplies. The guys told me that the only way to get anything was to trade for it. I asked them what they used for trading. It was a short conversation and it was even clearer that we didn't have anything worth trading.

Walkway

The guidelines provided a number of manuals to ensure each unit was in compliance. A TOA, or Table of Allowance, provided a list of approved items for each unit, depending on whether it was a squad, company, battalion or brigade.

Although this was covered in my training at Ft. Lee, it became more relevant when applied in a real setting. This system allowed a specific list of items and quantities for clothing, weapons, jeeps, diesel engines and more, based on the number of troops.

For larger and more expensive items, the Army published TMs, or Technical Manuals, providing guidance on how items worked, repair methods and required spare parts. A Prescribed Load List, or PLL, tracked the number of weapons and amount of ammunition. When the stock was down to a specified amount, the PLL indicated that it was time to reorder to ensure the items were always in stock.

When I arrived, the system that was used for tracking orders consisted of eight five-inch wide binders that covered the top of a desk. These binders included several single sheets of paper and three to seven IBM paper cards stapled to each page. This was unwieldy and difficult to track an order.

I closely followed my supply manual, the AR 735-35, to implement the supply system. I read this manual front to back to fully understand the process. Further research revealed that the codes on the cards often meant that the order was not allowed, on back order, or canceled as they had to be ordered at least three times in a ninety-day period.

In place of the numerous binders that covered the entire top of a desk, I established a single card file about eight inches wide and twelve inches deep. I set up a summary sheet of all orders and kept it in one small binder that provided an update on each order. As we received items, they were recorded correctly.

In my first month I asked the guys what they needed most and discovered that many didn't have bed sheets and they were sleeping on a bare mattress. I ordered my supplies from a depot about two miles away and we had to account for anything that was part of our allowed supplies. I went to the depot and asked how I could get some sheets. They said to get new stuff, I had to turn in used or old items. I didn't have any to turn in since they had been fully used. But they were still required in order to get new ones. I was in a Catch-22 situation.

I asked the guys from the depot what they did with the old sheets if I had them to turn in. They said they burned them and pointed to a pile of burned items. I asked them if they could pretend that I turned them in and they pretend that they burned them. They shrugged their shoulders in agreement and I picked up a hundred sets of sheets. That made a lot of guys happy. Once I understood the process, I got just about everything I wanted.

Some of the supply sergeants I inherited liked to keep supplies close to the vest, that is, they were reluctant to give stuff to the troops. Some guys had no socks or shirts and their underwear was full of holes and not given new ones when requested. I taught the supply sergeants how to use the system and told them to honor requests and reorder as needed. I used the system as designed, and within a few months, we filled our large warehouse with critical items such as soap, eating utensils, drinking glasses, bedding, clothing, mosquito nets, toilet paper, small generators and oil.

I enjoyed my work and soon made an impact on operations by providing needed supplies, using the well established but not often fully utilized Army supply system. We soon garnered a reputation for having stuff and provided requested items to each of our companies and had some left over for other units in need. Our goal was to make life easier and enjoyable for the troops.

A sergeant from brigade in Saigon called and asked me if I had any drinking glasses. We reported to brigade and they sent us notices telling us what to do and when, similar to a corporate headquarters. I told him we had them and to come on up.

When he arrived on a chopper, he explained that he was the brigade supply sergeant and could not fill the requests for his superiors and he was in a bind. This surprised me as we got our directives from Saigon where he was located. I gave him cases of plastic and glass glasses, plus knives, forks and spoons along with other supplies. He walked around our warehouse and picked out items like a kid in a candy store. He was very appreciative as he loaded up his chopper. I am sure he was going to be like Santa Claus when he returned.

Once, we got a notice to turn in all C-rations with a certain termination date. I loaded them on the two-and-a-half ton truck and hauled them out to the depot. We fork-lifted my current ones off and loaded on the new ones. I took them back to the battalion and we unloaded them by hand. Boy, we were proud that we had the current C-rations, even though we didn't eat them much in the rear. When we opened them, we discovered that they were older than the ones we turned in. I reversed the process and got our previous ones back. The system worked, but not always perfectly. Early in the Vietnam War, some C-rations were dated from World War II.

In my first year, virtually every day was the same as the one before. We got up about 6:30 to shower, ate breakfast and got to work by 7:30. The first order of the day during the dry season was to wipe the dust from the top of our desks. In the evening, we packed our work in our desks so it wouldn't be covered with dust the next morning.

We wore olive green fatigues, our standard military uniform, with pant legs tucked under at the top of our boots held by an elastic band. In the summer, we wore t-shirts in the office but were required to put on our shirts when outside or to the mess hall, topped off with a cotton hat. In short, it would be consistent with today's business casual. We wore flak jackets, helmets and carried weapons during a rocket attack, an alert or special drill.

There were about six truck drivers who convoyed to Qui Nhon, Cam Ranh Bay, Nha Trang, Saigon and other locations transporting supplies to us or to our outlying units. The timing of their return wasn't predictable due to fighting and ambushes. The truck drivers were warned against stopping at villages to buy sodas as rumor had it that drinks could be poisoned. They were also warned that women had razor blades in their vaginas and cut guys during sex. I don't know how that would work but I heard it.

After returning from a three- to five-day trip, they dropped off their goods in a number of ways. Since we didn't have a fork lift, we simply unloaded boxes by hand, or backed up the truck real fast and then hit the brakes and the item would slide off the back. I thought they would bring down our warehouse, but it survived.

During the day, we listened to popular music over Armed Forces Radio from disc jockeys similar to the ones back "in the world." They played the end of the year top 100 songs and *Sugar, Sugar* by the Archies was number one in 1969. We listened when the Celtics won the NBA championship, again. Television was limited, but I watched the fuzzy picture and listened when Kansas City won the Super Bowl.

We read the daily newspaper, *Stars & Stripes*, which provided a view of current events. This included sections on the stateside political and topical news, sports, and information on the war to include the on and off again negotiations.

We staggered the staff during lunch so someone was always available. I always said that lunch and dinner was great as it was one less meal I had to eat before I was going home. I preferred the terms lunch or dinner rather than chow, which sounded unappealing.

I had a good working relationship with the guys in the mess hall. We provided the supplies they needed and they rewarded us with evening comfort food like bologna, cookies or a sheet cake. Yes, bologna was a favorite as we didn't always get enough to eat, and there wasn't a Burger King open late.

One of my favorite treats during the hot season was to stop by the mess hall about 3:00 in the afternoon to have a cool glass of milk. The milk sat in the coolers for a couple hours and was cold while the milk served during regular meals was often warm.

To maintain our professional appearance, we got a haircut and a shave every two weeks for 75 cents--that included a shampoo and shoulder massage. Vietnamese men were the barbers and a woman provided the shampoo and shoulder massage. One night there was an attack on the perimeter and the attacker was the barber who had a sharp razor in his hand earlier that day.

Keeping up with the work load required us to work every day and well into the evening. On Sunday, those that wanted to attend church service did so then worked in the afternoon. We had time to chat during work and share stories of our life prior to the military.

Occasionally, we heard artillery fire over our buildings. Artillery Hill was only a couple miles from our base so when they fired overhead, it shook the buildings, and it was loud. Not sure if it was "incoming" or "outgoing," many ducked beneath their desks. After awhile, we knew, but the new guys took cover.

MACV (Military Assistance Command, Vietnam) was located a hundred yards down the road and was part of the first entrants into Vietnam in the early sixties. MACV had the best facilities with a theater outfitted with speakers and comfortable stateside type seats with a graduated slope to make the viewing more enjoyable. They also had a miniature golf course, basketball court, swimming pool and tennis courts. We had access to these facilities.

The NCO, Noncommissioned Officers, club was a place to have a beer or soda and hang out. NCOs were those with a grade of sergeant or above. The EM or Enlisted Men's club was larger and where shows were held. Bands with girl singers from Korea or the Philippines performed monthly, mostly covers of American songs.

Wearing regular clothes after work was optional. I often took advantage to feel more like a civilian for a little while. During a show, one of the "guards" tried to keep order and touched a guy on the shoulder and asked him to settle down. Unfortunately, the black guard tapped a white guy from Alabama. The Alabama guy was so incensed that he went back to his barracks to get his weapon and threatened to shoot the black guy. I was summoned by one of the guys, who said the guy was out of control. I went to the barracks to talk to him and he said, "Where I come from, a black man doesn't touch a white man." I said that if he was serious, I would have to call the MPs to arrest him. After about an hour he calmed down.

Another southerner who worked in the generator shop was a member of the KKK, and proud of it. We talked about the usual white domination crap, and he was convinced he was right. To put this in perspective, this was 1969 and the SEC was the only football conference without blacks participating.

I was assigned guard duty about every six weeks, sitting in the HQ bunker or in the adjoining battalion headquarters answering phone calls. The first night I pulled guard duty, while looking at all the telephones, microphones, and weapons in the bunker, the lieutenant in charge told me to flip a switch to turn on the lights, but I flipped the wrong switch. The siren went off, and the entire compound starting running to the bunkers. Eventually, we got everyone back to normal, but they called me "chicken-switch Shaughnessy" for some time. Even the Colonel good-naturedly kidded me about it rather than reprimanding me. I appreciated his support.

Periodically, I received letters from my family and friends. Coincidentally, I received a letter from Mary Kay, a.k.a. Sis Nyland, whenever I pulled guard duty. It was nice of her to take the time to write and I will always appreciate her for that gesture. She updated me on friends and family, weddings, children born and early divorces. When she sent me a letter informing me that Libby was getting married, I had mixed emotions. I considered sending her a letter asking her to wait for me.

But then I remembered that she didn't even wait for Christmas break before dating someone else, so there was little chance she was going to wait until I completed another two years of service. Finally, I decided that she must like the guy and it was best for me to simply stay out of the way.

Jim Nyland also sent letters and one came in an envelope with several couple's initials grouped together inside hearts. They represented couples that had to get married, i.e. knocked up.

We went to the perimeter bunkers in response to rockets shot by the enemy into friendly compounds, or as a precautionary measure. I was assigned an M-60 and M-16 for the bunker. The M-60 was heavy and used a belt of bullets stored in a can. After setting up the weapons, we assigned guys to watch. We also brought playing cards and a flashlight to catch up on poker and other games to pass time.

One night, a trip flare went off and artillery from about two miles away started shooting into our perimeter area. In the morning, we discovered that a cow had wandered into the area and there wasn't enough left to make a hamburger.

Another night, we witnessed the enemy invading a village. From our vantage point at the top of the hill we watched the firefight. Soon, gun ships were in the air and the NVA retreated into the night. We had to be careful observers as one guy who was watching got hit in the chest with a stray bullet and it killed him.

Each evening, about twenty soldiers stood at attention and were inspected for duty. As part of this ritual, the officer in charge inspected their "shined" shoes, clean weapons and he provided the daily password. Those at corporal or below were assigned to guard duty manning the towers along the perimeter of our compound while other guards walked the areas to ensure each vital location was protected from enemy intrusion. The perimeter had four guard towers that were occupied each night by those on guard duty.

Guard Tower

They answered questions on topics such as the names of the current president, battalion commander and other current events. The person who was most proficient would be on call, that is, not assigned a specific post but remained nearby in the barracks in case they were needed. A guy in our unit was usually the guy on call.

Knowing the daily password was important. No one could gain entry to certain areas without it. One night, a lieutenant approached a guard tower and started to climb the stairs. The guardsman said appropriately, "Halt, what is the password?" The lieutenant replied, "Sergeant, this is Lieutenant Smith, and I forgot the password." The guardsman replied, "If you take one more step up that ladder, I will blow you away."

The lieutenant tried to pull rank, but the guardsman remained vigilant and the lieutenant finally walked away to get the password. Of course, the lieutenant couldn't reprimand the soldier as forgetting the password would embarrass the officer.

Once, a shot was fired and we all hastened to find out the problem. Were we under attack? Did we need to fire up the siren? Did we need to call the Air Force to send up the gun ships? No. It turned out one of the guys on guard duty was homesick and decided his ticket out was to shoot himself. It was a harmless flesh wound. We thought, this guy can't even shoot himself, how is he going to protect the rest of us?

One of my jobs was to ensure that each company had the "approved" amount of ammunition. I reviewed C Company in Kontum in anticipation of the Inspector General (I.G.) inspection. They had about five times the allotment for grenades, bullets, claymore mines and more. They said that they had been overrun during Tet in 1968 and had nearly run out of ammo, and nearly lost their lives. They were going to be prepared in case of another attack. When the major in charge of the I.G. came and questioned me on the amount of ammunition they had at Kontum, I told him the background and added, "You go tell them that they can't have that ammo." He just smiled.

Prior to the I.G. inspection, we experienced a problem with the motor pool guys, especially one guy who liked to exercise his petty power by adhering strictly to the rules. I asked a guy that worked in our office to go to the PX but he returned saying that the motor pool would not allow us to have a jeep. I called the guy over and he stated that one of the bulbs in the headlight was out. I explained that he should have those in stock, and we were asking for the jeep on a perfectly clear day. He wouldn't budge.

I asked him how he was doing in preparing for the upcoming I.G. inspection. Recently, I noticed that he had manuals that had nothing to do with equipment that he had and was missing some that he should have. He said that he was waiting for my preliminary report but I replied that I was too busy helping others more cooperative with us.

Since he was a stickler for detail and wanted to do well on the inspection, he came back shortly with the signed authorization for the jeep. I talked with the guy and reminded him that we were all just trying to serve our time and we should try to make life easier for each other. He lightened up and we got along much better.

We handled issues raised by the I.G. as quickly as possible. We were well prepared but wanted to be sure that any problems were downgraded to a minor offense. Senior officers were measured and promoted based on these reports and, since our colonel and warrant officer were good guys, we wanted to make them proud. When the report was issued, we passed with flying colors.

One rainy day, I was given a driving ticket for not coming to a complete stop. When I told my boss, CW2 Ives, he flew into action. He called his warrant officer friend in the MPs (Military Police) and had the ticket destroyed. To me, it meant nothing, but each little item was an issue as it affected their overall ranking.

Although it appeared that MPs had a pretty cushy job, I wouldn't want it. They had to investigate drug use, rapes, robberies, murder, suicide and pulled convoy protection duty to ensure trucks and supplies made it safely to their destination.

The PX, (Post Exchange) or general store was located about a mile away--a good walk on a nice day, but it was just a short ride in a jeep. We all made numerous stops at the PX especially when we got our monthly allowance. Each person received a monthly allotment of two cases of beer, soda and cigarettes and the store punched our card when we bought them. Toward the end of the month, guys were always scrambling to find others who had not used their allotment.

Guys returned from the PX and informed us when hot items were in stock. If we missed the items, they would be gone for at least another month. Small, portable refrigerators, fans and stereo equipment such as turntables, reel-to-reel players and portable radios sold quickly. I didn't buy a refrigerator as my first three roommates were short timers with less than ninety days and my next two roomies were cheap. I was too.

For 35 cents we could buy knock-off record albums and regular ones sold for about $2 each. The quality of the knock-offs was not very good, but we recorded them to a reel-to-reel tape and played them for hours. Albums by the Beatles, Rolling Stones and others were available but they didn't last very long.

My favorite item was large bags of M&Ms that were stacked on a shelf about six feet wide and three feet high. I typically bought about six large bags and ate them within a few days. Thankfully the PX ran out or I would have gotten sick of them.

I bought a pearl necklace from the PX for $52.50 and kept it until I gave it to my wife 14 years later as a wedding gift when it appraised for more than $1,200.

There was a softball field down by the PX and games were played in the evening and on the weekends in the summer much like back home. The colonel, a couple lieutenants and I played handball a few times a week at the Air Force base until they told us it was too dangerous to drive at night.

I spent some nights in the barracks reading magazines, books, and listening to music while talking with roommates or friends. Reading Catch-22, I laughed so hard that those nearby asked what was wrong with me.

To keep us cool during the summer I bought a portable oscillating fan for our room in the barracks. The office didn't have air conditioning either. I found that if I kept moving rather than just sitting still it would mitigate the impact of the heat. It was hot, and after a rain it could be sweltering, especially during the summer.

The winter months were chilly, sometimes with highs of fifty degrees during the day. We boarded up the windows to reduce the breeze and loaded up on blankets. Some wore pajamas and others had electric blankets sent from home.

Dateline Pleiku: Whenever there was fighting in the Central Highlands, II Corps, the news was sent out with the heading Pleiku. Between bombings in nearby Cambodia and the fighting of the 4th Infantry Division, there was always news from Pleiku. Watching or reading the news, it appeared that I was involved in a lot of fighting. The headlines overstated any potential harm for those of us not in combat. I sent letters home stating that I was not in harm's way.

The Ho Chi Minh Trail bordered Vietnam and was a launching pad for attacks into the Central Highlands and throughout South Vietnam. It was close to Pleiku so we strongly supported any action to prevent the war from expanding into our area of operations, including all bombings. The 4th Infantry Division was nearby but we heard stories of their search and destroy missions ending with a number of U.S. casualties.

Periodically, our convoys were held up until an area of fighting could be cleared out and we were told to avoid certain roads. We could move around the area rather freely, but there were days and weeks when we were cautioned to be extra careful. For some guys, this meant getting their jeep back inside II Corps by night fall, but for many of us it meant eating in the mess hall and a night at the movies.

Pleiku International Airport

Transport Plane

Co-Workers

Our organization ran smoothly due to the quality of people in our operation. There was Ralph Wear from Houston, Rudy Mesa and DeLaCruz from San Antonio, McLaughlin from Boston, and Louie McDonough from St. Louis. Later, Bill Burkhart, Bill Schweier, McFarland and others rotated through. We worked well together and we accomplished a lot.

Ralph Wear was the resident gambler who bet on anything-- poker, pool and even typing. He won more money in card games than he made from his military pay. Ralph was tall, about 6'2", combed his black hair back and was very proficient at his job.

For guard duty, he was chosen as the special guard, which meant that he didn't actually pull guard duty unless someone got sick. That honor went to the person who was well dressed and could best respond to questions from the duty officer.

Others didn't realize that he kept one outfit cleaned and pressed for guard duty only and studied the Stars & Stripes newspaper to keep abreast of current events.

He sent most of his paycheck to his wife and won enough money each month to cover what little he needed.

Ralph Wear & Susie

Ralph bought stereo equipment, cameras and other stuff from catalogs at very low prices and sent them directly home. He adopted a dog and named it after his wife, Susie.

"Mac" from Framingham, Massachusetts was a daring guy. He lived on the edge and nearly fell off it a few times. He was about 5'9", blondish, red wavy hair and a truck driver. One night, returning late from downtown Pleiku, he came bursting into our room saying he needed help. After the Vietnamese guard refused to let him in the compound, Mac punched the guard and floored the jeep, but some of the barbed wire gate got caught under it. We managed to get it out and nothing ever came of it.

Mac was talking with a new guy, asking him where he was from. What state? Massachusetts. What city? Framingham. What street? It turned out they grew up within three blocks of each other and had never met until Vietnam. Small world.

Some guys bought and kept small refrigerators in their rooms and stored beer and soda, cokes, or pop, depending on what part of the country you were from. Our neighbor had a refrigerator but he was a real cheap guy; "tighter than two coats of paint." If you ever offered to buy him a drink, he said, "No thanks, but I'll take the money." He went to the local "steam bath" and asked the prices for the extras. It was $30 for fornication, or "a shot of leg" as it was commonly called, $20 for oral sex and $10 for a hand job. He exclaimed, "Hell, I can go back and do it myself for nothing."

One evening, while Mac and I were lying on our bunks, Mac asked our cheap neighbor if we could buy a couple drinks from him for the going rate of 10 cents each. The neighbor paused and then said that he was out. Mac took his bayonet and shoved it through the plaster wall, right over the chest of our neighbor on his bed. After a brief pause, the neighbor said, "Do you want Pepsi or Coke?"

Mac smoked a lot and ran out toward the end of the month before he could get his allotment. He'd walk by all the rooms in the barracks and say, "Let's smoke and bullshit, I got the bullshit."

One day, about thirty days after I was in country, a guy showed up with a warm greeting from everyone. Turns out, Rudy Mesa had my job before he served his year and went back to the states for his remaining year.

He couldn't stand the strict regimen and the constant inspections so he opted to re-up for another six-month tour in Nam. He was a very likable guy. At about 5'6", he was thin but had a little paunch around the middle. He had no interest in his old job, and just wanted to get in a truck and travel to pick up supplies.

Mac, Pratt, Mesa, Roommates

Being a truck driver was good duty as far as these few crazy guys saw it. They could take off in a convoy for four- to six-day roundtrips. They picked up generators, large equipment, jeeps and many critical miscellaneous items.

They were supposed to drive in a convoy all the time which provided the necessary weapons and guards for security. However, our guys didn't always do things by the book. Sometimes they ran out of sunlight but kept driving in the dark instead of stopping. It's not like there were any Holiday Inns. They needed to know the territory and occasionally they got fired upon. Fortunately, no one was ever hit, but they often drove scared. They were on the road frequently, sometimes making back–to-back trips.

After about four months, Rudy was in need of an R&R. Rudy told me that he didn't think he should go because there was so much to do. I told him that if a rocket hit him tonight, we would go on and get along without him, so he should go on his R&R. Rudy selected Taipei.

Some GIs enjoyed the beauty of the landscape and the women of Taipei. They lined up girls and each day the guys picked the one they wanted and paid about $15 a day. One guy fell in love with his call girl and was prepared to write a letter to his fiancé stating that he was in love with a hooker. We talked him out of it.

Rudy had a great time and returned to work refreshed. He was my teammate when we played touch football in a grassy area between our work place and Personnel. He was fun, and would take good natured ribbing about being a "wetback."

Rudy, Barracks

Louie McDonough was not a lifer but he drank and smoked like one. He started the day with a cigarette and a Coke. Louie was a truck driver and spent a lot of time on the road. His claim to fame was saving tables whenever a show came to the NCO club. We each gave Louie about $2 and he went to the club about 2:00 in the afternoon and drank while saving two tables for us. He was like Dean Martin, a man who liked to drink his dinner. Later, about eight of us showed up about fifteen minutes before the show. We carried Louie outside so he could sober up to watch the show, or go back to the barracks to sleep it off.

After a few months, Bill Burkhart replaced Ralph Wear. Bill was from Tampa and one of the smartest guys we all met even though he was a college drop out. He wore glasses that he constantly pushed back up his nose. He was about 6'2", red hair and thin, but not skinny. CW2 Ives, our boss, said that Burkhart was the brightest guy he ever worked with in his service years. Bill could type, set up a filing system, and complete ten things in order of priority.

The smart one was also the cheapest person I ever met, even worse than my neighbor. He was in Vietnam for fourteen months, longer than the normal tour of duty, and he spent less than $200 even though he smoked. He ate a few of everyone's french fries, sipped a little soda from others and 'nursed' a single drink for an evening.

At the PX, Bill anguished over buying an album by John Sebastian of the Lovin' Spoonful. He loved the guy but was afraid his solo album would disappoint. As expected, he didn't like it and he complained for months about wasting $2.

Bill was also kind of clumsy. We ate lunch and dinner together daily. On our way back from the mess hall, there was about a fifteen-foot wide gap where the raised walkway gave way to the dirt. A stone stuck out of the ground a couple inches and Bill would stumble on that stone just about every time we walked by it.

He had an interesting perspective on issues, making for lively discussions during the evening hours. One evening we were talking about some medical problems others had and Burkhart remarked how well our body functions, describing the inner workings. We thought Burkhart should become a surgeon to use both his mind and his hands.

Bill Burkhart

Bill Schweier arrived from Portland, Oregon a little after Burkhart. Schweier was only five hours short of a master's degree in English. He was skinny, witty and fun. He was a former disc jockey during school and he often quoted some of his favorite lines when a song came on the radio such as, "As we climb those sound steps to sound success," or "A golden nugget because you really dug it."

Bill was an especially good typist and proud of it. One evening, about 9:00, a captain from HQ came over and requested we get someone to type a letter immediately. It was going to Brigade HQ and it needed to be correct. I told him that we could help. I went to the barracks and asked Schweier to come to the office.

He only had on his T-shirt and pants with no boots. The pant legs dragged in the dirt, barely covering his flip-flops. In those days, we didn't have sophisticated equipment and supplies; simply a typewriter and two sheets of paper with carbon paper attached. He took the letter and within minutes, typed it, and handed it to the captain. He started to walk out of the office when the captain said, "Wait a minute, I need to proofread this." Bill just looked at me with a smirk, turned and kept walking. He didn't make mistakes.

Other evenings we just sat around the office, drinking soft drinks, and arguing about rock and roll. That is, were the Beatles better than the Rolling Stones? Who really created the electric sound first? And so on.

Later in our tour, the work started to wind down and we were not so busy. Schweier made up Jeopardy questions during the day and we played at night.

Bill Schweier

Not all guys were successful. Henry was a bright black guy who drove one of the trucks in a convoy. When he wasn't driving, he often had time to himself and got mixed up with the wrong crowd. Overall, he was a good worker, but he used the race card when he wanted to get out of doing something. Each Sunday, we had a skeleton crew working that allowed other guys time to go to church and take some time off. I prepared a list of the staff in alphabetical order and each would take their turn covering the office. When Henry's turn came, he said that he was being discriminated against. I pointed out that the list had been published for weeks. He didn't like it, but even he couldn't argue the point.

Periodically, there were unannounced inspections of the barracks, primarily looking for drugs. One afternoon, the NCOs were told to block the entrances to the barracks for a search.

I was guarding a door when Henry walked by. Later, the inspectors found a homemade bomb in Henry's locker. He was charged and sent to a holding cell to wait for his trial.

The jail and court were located at Camp Enari, part of the 4th Infantry Division, about ten miles away, through downtown Pleiku. After the trial where he was found guilty, I escorted him to LBJ, Long Binh Jail, near Saigon, flying a C-130, wearing a .45 pistol. While escorting him, I asked him what the hell he was going to do with a bomb. I never got a good answer.

I told him that if he wanted to make a run for it, I wasn't going to shoot him. I was afraid that I would shoot my foot getting the pistol out of the holster, like Barney Fife. I heard he was sent to Ft. Leavenworth in Kansas. I liked Henry and hope that he got out of jail in a reasonable time and is doing well. It was a classic case of hanging around with the wrong crowd.

After I delivered Henry, I woke up the next morning in an army barracks in Saigon and saw a guy from the Personnel department. I said hello and thought nothing of it. When I returned to Pleiku, I mentioned it to the guys in Personnel and they said the guy was AWOL. I told them where I saw him and they went to Saigon and brought him back.

The refrigerator in the office was stocked with soft drinks and snacks. The office was the obvious meeting place in the evenings. Some guys spent their evenings drinking at the NCO or EM clubs, or going downtown for a shot of leg, among other activities. We hung around the office at night.

Occasionally, a guy from San Diego stopped by to chat. He had found God and was born again after being a drug addict or alcoholic. He was a short, pudgy blond haired Californian. He always generated discussions on religion.

Some guys had a lot of hookers in their rooms at night and they suffered from the clap so badly that they had to cancel their R&R with their wives and almost extended their tour in order to heal, almost.

These guys did not adhere to the PCOD, (see glossary) that set a date a guy should stop having sex before he was going on R&R to meet his wife or girl friend, or going home for good. Guys who had any type of disease, whether it was malaria or venereal, had to be cleared or they could not leave the country.

There were many others who were assigned to us and went through the supply system; some drivers, some worked in supply rooms and some were clerks. We were all fortunate to have good duty and nobody was harmed during their stay.

When guys left, we had a cookout to celebrate their leaving, typically on a Sunday afternoon. We had a large grill that we fired up, got some steaks and dessert from the mess hall, and a large cooler that kept the beer and sodas cold. We got French bread from downtown Pleiku and added some butter and garlic salt and toasted it on the grill. We bought the French bread even though we were warned that anything that we bought from the Vietnamese could be poisoned. Since we kept buying it, you could say that we loved the bread and would die for it.

It was a great time to share some highlights and lowlights of that person's time in Nam and hear of their future plans. Besides being a time to reflect on their time in Nam, it also gave the rest of us a pause to consider our situation and future. Of course, we all wanted to be on the same "freedom bird" taking that GI home.

Mark-busy at work

82

Superiors/Officers

All Officers are not created equally. At the top of the chart are West Pointers. They are well educated with good management and leadership skills. Next, are ROTC officers who gained experience with military policies during their college years. Graduates of Officers Candidate Schools (OCS) didn't require a college degree, and sometime it showed.

Army officers in order of ascending rank are second lieutenant, first lieutenant, captain, major, lieutenant colonel, colonel (full bird), and four levels of generals. The size of the commanding unit dictates what level officer is in charge. A company is typically led by a captain, a battalion by a lieutenant colonel and so forth. The lieutenant colonel was in charge of the 43rd Signal Battalion, commanding the three to six companies that were under his direct control. Our colonel was a very likable guy and ran a good operation.

He followed protocol, but was not hung up on the rules and regulations. In fact, I was lax in adhering to protocol. I did not always stand when he entered the room. I didn't always salute him when he walked by because I had read that we should not salute a superior officer in the open to avoid tipping off the enemy who the leader was.

The colonel developed a favorable impression of me since I was getting a lot of supplies for the officers, noncommissioned officers, enlisted men and the outreaching companies. We got everything from utensils and comfort items like sheets, socks and underwear to the valued rain jackets during the monsoon season. I gained personal satisfaction from providing the needed supplies to the guys and it gave some relief to the soldiers while away from home. One day in November 1969 the colonel and the captain came into our work area and we all jumped to attention. I was singled out with "Attention to Orders," and promoted to staff sergeant, SSG, E-6. I was delighted that my hard work was noticed.

I later learned from a guy in Personnel how the colonel commanded it to happen. I appreciated him taking such extraordinary steps to make it a reality. Previously, the colonel approached the Personnel department saying that he wanted to promote me from sergeant E-5 to staff sergeant, E-6. He was told the criteria for promotions: the soldier must have at least three years in the current grade and seven years in the Army. Since I only had nineteen months in service and barely sixteen months in grade, I was not a qualified candidate based solely on the Army criteria. However, the colonel didn't care and just told them to do it.

I didn't hear of any resentment for my promotion as I had gained a reputation for getting things for a lot of people. The system was working and the warehouse was full of items and they were not just stored there, but were shared among those that needed them. My pay increased another $40 a month to nearly $300. But the promotion had its drawbacks. Higher command often approached me to procure unusual items.

The Executive Officer (XO), second in command of the battalion, was a major and a West Point graduate. He called me into his office and asked me to get him a .50 caliber gun that mounts on the back of a jeep or truck. He wanted to put it on our truck so we could move our supplies without waiting for a convoy. I told the major that it was not on our TOA, Table of Allowance, but he felt that, with my connections, I could get one. I never got the .50 caliber machine gun, and avoided the major whenever possible. I don't recall how long he was there before I arrived, but he rotated out before long.

The reality was that there were too many officers to fill the few slots available to command. And, during war time, the way to get promoted is to get command time. As a result, officers were often rotated in and out of command positions every six months rather than serving a full year in their job. This meant that field soldiers and clearly the more experienced NCOs often understood the operation and battlefield conditions far better than their superiors.

I had some interaction with the captains in our battalion headquarters and in the field with favorable results. For the most part, they seemed to do a good job. Of course, the captain that gave me my promotion was my new best friend. The captain in charge of A Company was a pain.

Lieutenants in the rear were clearly less important than Warrant Officers and many of the NCOs they commanded. To be fair, those who took ROTC during college were more knowledgeable and experienced than those that went through Officers Candidate School (OCS). OCS was a means for those with a high school education, or some college, but no ROTC training, to become an officer. Some of these "90 Day Wonders" were simply not prepared for their responsibilities.

While I was considering OCS, I was told that second lieutenants were likely to lead troops into battle and thus the most expendable leaders. My experience with lieutenants was limited, since I worked in the rear, so it is unfair for me to categorically comment on all of them. In fact, many lieutenants died valiantly; leading, protecting or saving their men in combat.

Many of the lieutenants that served in the support area seemed to want to serve as little time as possible in the Army and stay out of the way. In supply, lieutenants often signed for their property books, or inventory, without checking to make sure the items were there. If an officer signed for items and they were missing when he left, he was personally liable for replacing it or paying for it out of his final pay check. Some took a chance and hoped that others would come in and sign for the stuff like they did without taking inventory. One officer in our unit was simply unaware of his responsibility, and blindly signed for a large number of items that were missing.

A lieutenant from A Company, which was located on the same compound as the battalion, asked me to review what he might be liable for as he was approaching his DEROS, Date Eligible for Return from OverSeas. After my initial review, I discovered several jackets, equipment and other miscellaneous items missing totaled about $800. He said that it wasn't that important and left.

He was hoping that someone would be as sloppy as him and simply sign for the missing items. A couple days later he had a change of heart and stopped by and asked me if I could help him. I had some excess items and got supplies to replace his missing stuff. He thanked me and went home with no out-of-pocket expenses.

I spent more time with a lieutenant assigned to battalion than others. I drove him to Camp Enari during Henry's court martial for having a bomb in his locker. Although I liked the guy, he got on the backs of others and they didn't like him. When his time came to leave, I asked the guys about a party for him, but nobody wanted to make the effort to put together a cookout. I was a little embarrassed for him as he clearly expected a farewell party.

Warrant Officers are the experts, the glue that holds the Army together. They specialize in supply, finance, personnel, motor pool and other specialties. They are career guys who become proficient in an area, much like an accountant, HR person, or other counterparts in corporate life. Warrant Officers are also helicopter pilots but more information will be provided on them later.

Chief Warrant Officer, CW2 Ives, from Peru, had been in the military for more than twenty years and was going for thirty. He knew the book on supply and when he arrived a couple months after me, he added knowledge and experience to our organization. He was our boss and held everyone accountable, but did so in a friendly way and showed appreciation for good work.

When CW2 Ives came on board, he took a thorough inventory and found a number of items missing or incomplete. Some cases had nothing inside, like a computer without a hard drive. After Ives completed his review, he gave me a list of missing items and asked me to find them.

I began the search and was able to replace many of them. I obtained items through the system, or I called in favors from other supply guys. I then gave them to Ives and started to tell him how I got the stuff. He held up his hands, stopping me from telling him how I did it. He didn't want to know.

In addition to being great to work for, Ives also helped me out of a touchy situation. The Vietnamese women who did our laundry and shined our boots were paid on a weekly basis. One week, a laundry worker, Dong, was having her wisdom teeth taken out and had worked it out to be absent for two days with others doing her work. However, she was only paid for three days work, not five days, and she called on me to help her. We paid the corporal in charge of the program $5 and he, in turn, paid the Vietnamese.

The corporal refused to pay her, saying she didn't work the full five days even though she had others fill in and the guys were satisfied with the work. He said that since she didn't do the work, she wasn't going to be paid. I recommended that he should return the money to the guys so we could pay her. He didn't agree. The real reason he was upset was that the girl in question had a very attractive sister, and she refused to set up this guy with her.

Since he refused to pay, I informed him that I was taking it to a higher authority. I went to the lieutenant in charge of the company but he took no action, looking down at papers on his desk while I was talking. It was a classic case of someone who didn't want to ruffle any feathers, just put in his time and move on.

I then went to his superior, a black captain, and appealed the decision. The captain said that he gave the corporal the responsibility so with that he also gave him the authority. I said that the reason we have superior officers is to ensure those below them use their authority properly. He should be aware of how unjust it is to make indiscriminate decisions affecting those who have little or no recourse. He remained firm in his decision. I was prepared to take this up the chain of command to the battalion commander, but I wanted to go through the proper channels.

I was talking with the guys in the office about the situation when Ives overheard my comments. He called his warrant officer friend in Personnel and I relayed the story to him. The Personnel warrant officer called me back within an hour and explained that the Vietnamese worker would get paid. He said that the corporal was warned and if he repeated the action, he would be reprimanded.

A few days later, the captain walked through our office and he said to me in front of others, "You lost the battle, but won the war." I felt satisfaction in using the process and getting a positive outcome.

Although lieutenants technically outranked warrant officers, they were no match for warrant officers' knowledge. In some instances, lieutenants were foolish enough to suggest that CW2 Ives do something because they outranked him. He informed them that he would be happy to arrange a meeting with the colonel to discuss the matter. Ives was steadfast and was not going to do anything that was improper that put him or others in a compromising role. He supported our efforts and backed us up when challenged. Of course, we had to be right.

Our sergeant major was a good guy and we got along great. He was reasonable in his requests and wouldn't ask for anything that was illegal. He wanted stuff to help out the troops and that was hard to deny. Each week, he flew a chopper to our different company locations throughout the Central Highlands. One week, he came back and told me that Kontum was out of eating utensils. He asked me to send out some forks and spoons.

The Vietnamese who worked in the kitchen stole them by putting them in the garbage. When other Vietnamese took the garbage to the dump, they went through it and sorted out the utensils, cleaned them up and either took them home or sold them.

A chopper was not to make another trip until the following week, and a convoy was not scheduled. I suggested that he take the utensils on his next weekly trip. I threw in extra cases of glasses; the plastic ones for the enlisted men and the glass ones for the officers and senior enlisted. He was welcomed on his next visit.

He asked me to get him some paint. I told him I wasn't authorized to get it, but he wasn't deterred, reminding me that we weren't authorized all the sports supplies either. He kept asking me why I wasn't getting him paint. I told him that if I got it, we would have to paint something, and everyone would be on my back for providing it. He promised that he would wait three months before painting, and he would say he got it from Saigon.

He helped me get an early promotion, so I got him the paint. Two weeks later, everyone was painting buildings, jeeps and anything that had a smudge. I asked him about the three month wait, and he mumbled something about the coming monsoon season being a mere four months away.

I nearly caught hell once for taking care of my sergeant major friend. Occasionally, I umpired softball games. In the only game the sergeant major played, he hit one down the left field line. It was foul by about two feet but I called it fair. As the opposing team captain came after me, pulling rank, of course, I simply told him that the sergeant major only played one game a year and he needed a break. I promised a favor to his team during the game. He walked away. The sergeant major stayed on second with a double.

I traveled throughout the region to check on each company, secure supplies or for R&R and leave. The C-130 airplane was the common form of travel. Sometimes, the planes' windows were left open, whether intended or not. As we took off on one flight, we heard a loud bang. The pilot had not closed his window and it flipped closed rather abruptly. Air travel was not always predictable. Flights were delayed or cancelled without notice. Occasionally, I slept in a corner of an airport on a cement floor with my knapsack as a pillow.

Although I typically flew C-130s, flying in helicopters was a more direct route and was kind of fun. The pilots told me that it was difficult, if not impossible, for a person to fall out of a helicopter due to centrifugal force. Thus, when we heard of one of two enemy soldiers falling out of a chopper at 2,000 feet, it was viewed with skepticism. Most likely, it was to encourage the other guy to talk about enemy positions.

Some warrant officers flew their choppers in combat zones. Other helicopter pilots had better assignments like those who flew our commanders to base camps each week. The pilots had a reputation for being a bit on the wild side. Warrant officers flew the sergeant major on his weekly visits to different companies. Our sergeant major was strict in adherence to the military order. He got after these free spirits about the long length of their hair.

On one trip, the pilots flew low to the ground and headed toward trees that lined the road. The sergeant major started yelling for them to pull up. As they neared the trees, they turned the chopper sideways to pass by them. The pilots told me later that he treated them very nicely after that incident or the next time they would have taken the chopper to 2,000 feet and cut the engines.

Air travel was dictated by the weather and the enemy. The monsoon rains made it difficult to fly helicopters. They had to fly at a relatively low altitude and could be shot at from the ground like ducks flying across the sky. They had to fly at 1,500 feet to remain above the reach of small arms fire. I got fired on a couple times, but I still favored chopper travel to all others.

One day, I was visiting the nearby hospital to get my regular six-month shots and I heard that they were bringing in a wounded soldier. I watched as they opened up the MASH-like van and brought him into the room. He was surrounded by doctors and nurses, some sticking needles into him as others were cutting off his clothes. He was shot just below the heart. I don't know if he made it, but I know they did the best they could for him. I gained an up close look at what the war does to a human being.

While at the hospital, I recognized an attractive nurse, recalling her from my last visit when she was new. At that time she hesitantly asked departing soldiers if they had any medical problems or venereal disease. This time, she came out and said, "Any of you guys had the clap?" A little experience shortens the time to get to the heart of the matter. They said if one shot of penicillin wouldn't kill the VD, then a second one would. We could tell if someone had Gonorrhea, or the clap. They walked a little funny, kicking one leg out as they would be "dripping" to alleviate the discomfort.

Since our everyday interaction with females was of the small Vietnamese women who weighed about seventy-five pounds, American nurses appeared as Amazons in comparison. It was rumored that some of the nurses made more money in illicit off duty activities than regular pay. However, if it occurred, they were discreet and they only fraternized with higher paid officers.

But, as I said, this is just a rumor. Regardless of the rumors, nurses played a vital role in caring for those seriously wounded and the rest of us. About 10,000 Army nurses served in Vietnam, and we owe them our gratitude. Unfortunately, eight military and fifty-six civilian women lost their lives in Vietnam.

To avoid the hospital, we were encouraged to take malaria pills. When we first arrived, we took them regularly. But they were large enough to be labeled horse pills. Soon, very few took them as we never heard of guys getting the dreaded disease. It seemed that more guys choked on the pills than got malaria.

On Christmas Day, 1969, I had firsthand experience with the medical unit. We celebrated Christmas with a full lunch of turkey, mashed potatoes and cranberry sauce with pumpkin pie for dessert. Like others, I was taking it easy that afternoon, just lying around the barracks. About 5:00, a few of us decided to head back to the mess hall to get some dinner. As I was walking across the open area between the barracks and the mess hall, I felt a twinge of pain in my right side. It wasn't sharp, rather a dull but persistent pain.

I tried to walk it off, but by the time I got to the building that housed a pool table, I had to lie down on it. I waited another five minutes before I asked one of the guys to get a jeep to take me to the medical unit down the street. When I arrived, I was placed on a bed and waited for the doctor. He examined me and thought it was kidney stones. I asked him to give me something for the pain, but he said he couldn't because then he wouldn't know if it passed. He was about to administer a thick liquid into my bloodstream to dislodge the kidney stone when I motioned that I was about to throw up, which I did with great passion.

After a few minutes, the doctor shot some liquid through me. Within thirty minutes I felt the pain and discomfort leave. I used a screen to catch the kidney stone when I urinated as the doctor wanted to send it to Saigon for analysis. Fortunately, for the remainder of my tour, I didn't have to use the medical facilities and only went there for my six month shots, R&R, leave, or when departing "back to the world."

Laundry Women

School Children

Vietnamese People

The Vietnamese women were hard workers and could be relied upon to show up for work. They didn't make much money, but it was steady work and beat pulling up rice. They were like others throughout the world; they wanted to be happy, to have good relationships with others, and enjoy their family.

Each week day, Vietnamese women from Pleiku were brought in to do our laundry. Our guy in charge of the women drove a deuce-and-a-half truck and the women jumped on the back. When the day was done, they were taken home. Sometimes, Vietnamese hookers jumped on the truck that delivered the other workers each day and the hookers spent the day or night. Kind of like pizza delivery, by the piece.

We had enough sets of fatigues to have a clean set each day, but not much to spare. Since our pants and shirts were marked with our names, we got them back correctly. But, underwear and socks, especially socks, were often mismatched.

When I first arrived, I had six new pair of socks. By the end of the first week, I had one of the original new pairs. I told the gal that I expected to get them back, and tried to pin them together so she would recognize mine, but to no avail. I was fortunate that I was in charge of supplies and could get more of just about everything, but there wasn't an unlimited supply.

My laundry girl, Lam, was engaging and despite the language barrier, we were able to effectively communicate. She was a nice young gal and was the contact person for the remainder of the laundry women and wasn't afraid to tell me when she needed supplies.

Lam, Hooch girl

With Vietnamese, if something was positive, it was "number one," but a negative was "number ten." Of course, I was a number ten until they wanted something, then I was number one. When I passed by the barracks, Lam yelled out "number ten, number ten," and I ignored her. Then she yelled "number one" and I turned around and smiled. She usually wanted soap.

If they agreed with what you said or wanted, they simply said, "no sweat GI." If you asked them to do something that had been done before, they nodded their heads and said, "yeah, same, same."

The Vietnamese people were small, often weighing in the range of sixty-five to a hundred pounds for a larger male. It was unusual if they went over a hundred pounds due to their diet and genetics. Vietnamese kids were smiling and friendly. Whenever we interacted, the kids touched our arms to feel the hair as they had no hair on their own.

The Vietnamese lived under terrible conditions. The living quarters were primitive, consisting of tin roofs with cardboard siding and dirt floors with no plumbing. When it rained they showered under the roofs' water run off. The houses were close to each other, much like a ghetto. The movie *Slum Dog Millionaire* reminded me of the squalor.

Pleiku Suburbs

Vietnamese women wore their traditional black pajama bottoms with a slit shirt covering part or all of their trousers, known as ao dai. In the winter time, they were at the mercy of the weather and had little 'shelter from the storm.'

Vietnamese women were cute, and some were pretty. However, those of French descent were striking in their beauty. They were perfectly shaped and their facial features were more angular. Our drivers always welcomed a trip to Ban Me Thuot, (Bay me to it) located about ninety miles south of Pleiku. The French had a long term stronghold there that produced beautiful women. They were more refined and unwilling to sell a shot of leg for any amount of money. There was a story of a GI who was so obsessed with a woman that he married her just to sleep with her, and then left her behind when he returned to the states.

Downtown Pleiku had a market place where they sold fish (I didn't say fresh catch). The fish stunk and the flies didn't add to its appeal. In fact, when driving through Pleiku, I braced for the smell of garbage. There were no street sweepers and it is unlikely there was garbage pick up.

One of the worst smells was that of "nuoc mam," so gross that I was sickened by it. Nuoc mam is made by putting fish in kegs with a salt layer and water and left in the sun for months. The juice from this mixture is drained from the bottom and is a sauce for their rice and other foods.

While I was at the supply depot at lunch time, waiting for the crew to return, the Vietnamese women workers were eating lunch, dipping rice in this foul smelling sauce. I asked them if they liked it, thinking maybe they were eating this because they had nothing else to eat but they said it was all good. I left the waiting area and went outside as the smell almost made me throw up.

Montagnards, as the French called them, or people of the mountains, are unique to the Central Highlands and are made up of several different tribes with fundamentally the same, but slightly different, traditions. Known as "the Yards", they numbered about 750,000 to one million, and were spread across the Central Highlands with most of them in South Vietnam.

The North Vietnamese conscripted many of them to fight for them as did the U.S. Montagnards lived in South Vietnam, but other tribes were located in the North. Although they were peaceful people, they were notorious warriors throughout history. Montagnards joined the army and were known for taking no prisoners, that is, if you were caught, you were shot.

Ko Poe was a Montagnard who worked as our warehouse guy and would load and unload trucks while keeping the warehouse in order. He was strong for a guy that weighed about eighty pounds. He was a reliable worker and an overall good guy. When we gave him a ride to his village, the conditions were sparse. His hut had a mud floor and when it got cold, the five children huddled together and the ones on the ends would be cold.

When we received wooden crates protecting a generator or other large item, we loaded the wood or corrugated board and delivered it to Ko's village. Further, we provided blankets, clothing and other protective wear so they were more comfortable.

After several months working for us, Ko didn't show up for a week and we all wondered what happened to him. We went to his village, but they said he was gone. While driving down the road one day, I heard my name called. I stopped my truck, and Ko came running up to me. He told me that he had joined the army to help in the fight.

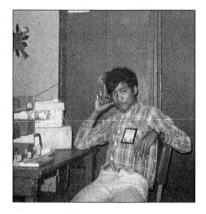

Ko Poe

96

Locally, we had a positive relationship with the Vietnamese people. However, in other parts of the country, relations between Americans and the Vietnamese people were often strained. Some GIs resented that we were there to fight for the freedom of the South, but some men our age appeared to be lazy and not engaged in battle or much of anything. In fact, it wasn't until 1968, under pressure from the U.S., that the South Vietnamese drafted eighteen year olds, while Americans at the same age had been serving in Vietnam for years. Derisive terms such as gooks, slopes and dinks were names given to the young men of South Vietnam. The older women and men were held in higher regard and referred to as mama-san and papa-san respectively.

The South Vietnamese farmers were unhappy with their treatment by American forces. Many Vietnamese people were removed from their land to refugee camps, losing their rice production, and men were forced into the military. They once had a thriving rice industry, exporting a considerable amount to the rest of the world and providing for their families and fellow villagers. During the war and a few years beyond, South Vietnam had to import rice, their natural commodity.

Although we were there to win the hearts and minds of the Vietnamese people, as President Johnson stated often, the reality was that we were alienating an equal number, especially those in villages located nearby the heavily fought areas. More egregious actions were taken toward the Vietnamese earlier in the war, particularly among those in the field. Those of us in the rear heard stories of GIs killing enemy soldiers and cutting off their ears as souvenirs. U.S. soldiers felt threatened when approached by children and women, not knowing if they were friendly or if they carried a hand grenade to blow themselves up along with GIs.

Food and weapons were stored in huts in the villages providing supplies for the Viet Cong. The civilians were under pressure from the NVA to go along with them. The U.S. instituted "Free Fire Zones," whereby the strategy was to relocate Vietnamese civilians to refugee camps and then destroy the villages with artillery and ground forces called "Zippo Squads."

However, some GIs failed to evacuate civilians and took their retaliation too far by simply killing anyone who moved. Dead animals were thrown into the wells to contaminate the water to discourage others from returning.

There was pressure on the field to report body count. It was the way to keep score of enemy dead. Quotas were established and some men shot civilians and reported that the enemy was fleeing. However, no weapons were found, and there were no casualties of U.S. soldiers making the "firefights" reported even more suspect. Stories of such atrocities were told back in the U.S. resulting in war protests by civilians. Some returning soldiers were called "baby killers" among other demeaning names. However, these unconscionable acts were attributed to very few soldiers.

Some renegade U.S. soldiers were killing the very people we were there to liberate. Another toll was the psychological impact on both the soldiers who committed the crimes as well as those who witnessed and reported them. These war crimes were well chronicled in the book, *Tiger Force* by Pulitzer Prize winners Michael Sallah and Mitch Weiss.

My Lai

Another event that led to Americans questioning the war strategy in the first year of Nixon's presidency was the massacre of Vietnamese civilians at My Lai. Although this event occurred in March 1968, the events would not be known for another year. This infamous act against civilians took place on March 16, 1968, when Charlie Company, 1st Platoon, led by Lt. William Calley killed, by official count, 347 South Vietnamese men, women and children in the village of My Lai. Lt. Calley was a product of OCS training, a "90 day wonder" and, regrettably, he was given a leadership position that he was not fully prepared for. He was from Columbus, Georgia and had flunked out of junior college.

Lt. Calley was leading a group of men that had been in country for about two months, and the villages they were assaulting were thought to be strongholds of the Viet Cong. The area was expected to be hot, so artillery fire and gun ships sprayed the area before the troops landed. Expecting heavy firing, they were told to "kill everything." Once the shooting started, with Lt. Calley leading in the killing, other solders joined in. GI's bayoneted civilians as they came out of their huts. They tossed hand grenades into huts, and lined up the villagers near a drainage ditch and shot them.

Some GIs protested, saying that this is not what they signed up for and that we were there to help these people, not kill them. During the shooting, Warrant Officer Hugh Thompson, who was searching for the enemy while flying a chopper, saw what was happening. He landed his chopper and confronted Calley, but was told that it was none of his business. Thompson, his gunner Larry Colburn and crew chief Glenn Andreotta, left but soon witnessed other civilians trying to escape.

Thompson set down the chopper and told the soldiers to stay put while he rescued the civilians. This act was later construed as Thompson threatening fellow soldiers. They discovered that a young baby was still alive in the ditch. They brought the child to a local orphanage supported by nuns who cared for the child.

Coincidentally, the two central characters of this event were both from Georgia. Hugh Thompson was from Stone Mountain, a suburb of Atlanta, and William Calley was from Columbus, about 100 miles away. Had they met under different circumstances, they would have likely been good friends.

Warrant Officer Hugh Thompson spent a number of years testifying before Congress, accused of insubordination and threatening other soldiers. He served 20 years in the military before retiring. Thompson, Larry Colburn, and the late Glenn Andreotta (killed two weeks after the My Lai incident), received the Soldier's Medal.

Apparently, commanders throughout the chain of command were aware of the slaughter, but did nothing about it. In fact, when some soldiers reported the incidents, they were ignored. Ron Ridenhour, a Vietnam veteran, wrote a letter to President Nixon, and a number of top level officials. Although Ridenhour was not at My Lai, he had heard the stories from his buddies. The letter was forwarded to General William Westmoreland who ordered a thorough investigation. This included a photographer who was at My Lai, Sergeant Ron Hoeberle, who had photos of the killings.

Calley admitted on the witness stand that he executed civilians, but he was acting on direct orders from his company commander. Twenty-six other American soldiers were charged, but only Calley was convicted on 22 counts of murder for the My Lai massacre and was given a life sentence. President Nixon reduced it and Calley only served two years under house arrest at Ft. Benning, Georgia. This story is detailed in the book, *The Forgotten Hero, The Hugh Thompson Story*, by Trent Angers.

In subsequent years, Calley has not talked about that day, but on August 19, 2009, Calley spoke at the Kiwanis Club of Greater Columbus, Georgia. During that speech, he said, "There is not a day goes by that I do not feel remorse for what happened that day in My Lai. I feel remorse for the Vietnamese who were killed, for their families, for the American soldiers involved and their families. I am very sorry." Perhaps, that is all we can ask of him at this time.

R&R. Hong Kong

During the first six months of my tour, I had developed a good working supply system, built some positive relationships with coworkers and supported the troops with supplies. Now, it was time to take a break. Soldiers were given a five- to seven-day R&R, Rest and Recuperation, after about five months of their tour of duty. We could choose from: Thailand, Japan, Taiwan, Singapore, the Philippines, Hong Kong, Sidney, or Hawaii. I selected Hong Kong.

Guys on R&R meet their wives or girlfriends usually in Hawaii. Typically, these encounters played out in one of three ways. First, they went and had a good time. Second, they went with the clap and gave it to their wife or girlfriend with dire consequences. Third, they went and came back with the clap, getting it from their wives or girl friends, and we laughed at them. Some guys cancelled their R&R at the last minute as they had the clap and didn't want their spouse to get it, or to find out they were fooling around. All of these options happened in our unit.

There were certain rules about going on R&R and most guys adhered to them. Be sure to have enough money ($200+), don't spend it all in the first night with the first hooker you meet, and stay away from hot spots that are provided on a map. I ran into a guy from our unit that broke every rule within twenty-four hours. I reluctantly gave him some money to get him through the week.

I decided to buy some custom fitted clothes to take advantage of Hong Kong's world specialty and save some money. I felt all the cloth, and picked out shirts and slacks. They promised they would have the clothes finished by the time I left.

The salesmen took me out to dinner at a Chinese restaurant. I tried the chop sticks, wanting to be like the locals. However, when the food came, the local guys shoveled the food into their mouths with the chop sticks. They didn't like using chop sticks any more than I did.

I ate at one of Hong Kong's finest restaurants, The San Francisco Steak House and it was great. Hong Kong was a beautiful city and just walking around was a welcome departure from Pleiku.

The next day I started my tour with buying a number of expensive rolls of film. I started on the Star Ferry, operating for nearly a century, across Victoria Harbor between Hong Kong and the Kowloon Peninsula. The Victoria Harbour is one of the deepest maritime ports in the world. Crossing the bay, I noticed a number of boat people who lived on them all the time; not trusting the land.

Once across, I took the Peak Tram, a vertical rail transport between Central and Victoria Peak that had been in service for more than a century. The Peak Tram provided a panoramic view of Hong Kong. I took a lot of pictures going up and down the hill and of the Victoria Harbour. At the end of the tour, a guy was selling package of slides for $2 of the very same shots I took but at a much greater cost to me.

Hong Kong consists of Hong Kong Island, Lantau Island, Kowloon Peninsula, the New Territories and some 260 islands. Hong Kong has little arable land and few natural resources and must import food and raw materials. It was a British Colony from 1842 until they transferred sovereignty to China in 1997. The agreement stipulates that Hong Kong operate with autonomy until 2047.

Some citizens feared the take over and left for the U.S. and other democratic neighboring countries. It appears there was a benefit to this merger of unequals as China has clearly become an international trade force, often using their own rules, but being effective in the process.

The clothes were not ready when I left and they promised to send them to me.

Back to Vietnam

I felt refreshed after I arrived back from the Hong Kong R&R, and was ready to get back to work for another six months remaining in my tour. I received my clothes within a couple weeks and they were all too small.

On a local level, the monsoon season had started and it rained virtually every day and so hard that we could barely see in front of our faces. The ditches were three feet wide and deep and often filled to capacity. We constantly scraped off the mud between the grooves in the bottom of our boots. The rains made it difficult to travel the paved roads and impossible on the unpaved ones.

The rain usually let up for a two-hour period each day from about 1:00 to 3:00 in the afternoon and that is when I ran my errands, usually to the supply depot. A new officer got on my back because he wanted me to run an errand in the morning and insisted we do it then. I followed orders and he was riding and I was driving the two-and-a-half ton truck back from the depot about 11 a.m. It started to rain so hard that we could not see the road in front of us. We turned off to a side road and waited until the rain slowed. He never told me when to do anything again.

We were also pleased that the engineers put in indoor plumbing in the same building opposite the sinks and around from the showers. Now we could go to the bathroom in front of everyone, but we could do it under better conditions, I think. There's nothing more appealing than watching others take a crap while shaving right after a shower.

Our supply guys were put in charge of a number of tasks. Fire extinguishers were often in need of refill, particularly where the senior NCOs lived. Our own Sergeant Wilson (right), said that they used the fire extinguishers to put out their grills each evening. War is hell.

I was also in charge of signing off on all cartons of stuff that were sent home. The normal items included clothes, stereo equipment and gift items, but I also saw machetes, .45 caliber pistols, knives and drugs. Although I was supposed to report these infractions, I simply asked the GIs to remove the contraband and then I signed off. I didn't have the time to fill out more paperwork, and I didn't want to delay guys from getting home. I had to witness the closing and sealing of the containers but I wondered if, after I left, the guys who worked in the shipping area simply opened the boxes and stuffed illegal items into it and shipped it.

This occurred near the PX, and although I didn't always welcome the interruption, it gave me an excuse to visit the PX to see what new items had come in.

The biggest problem I had was getting oil for the motor pool. It required me driving a two-and-a-half ton truck several miles to a depot and then carting several barrels back. It wouldn't have been so bad except the guys in the motor pool gave me less than a day's notice before they ran out. Plus, as mentioned, the guy was a pain in the neck. But, I shouldn't complain. Many had it worse than me.

In fact, those of us in the rear knew we had good duty. We were empathetic toward the guys in the field. Of course, we were willing to put in the extra year to avoid the infantry, although some still saw plenty of action. Based on the history of the Central Highlands and Pleiku, we would have expected to see more action. We were lucky.

I see movies where supply sergeants seem to make a lot of money dealing in contraband, but I never had much opportunity. I couldn't see making much money selling mattresses.

During my first year in-country, there were a number of changes occurring on the political front that kept us guessing as to what would happen in Vietnam. There were actions and decisions made in Vietnam that would impact how the politicians in Washington viewed the progress of the war, but we were unsure how it would impact us on a local level and the war in general. We were aware of these issues and, over time, gained more insight on the details that provided a backdrop for the war strategy.

When Nixon took office in January 1969, there were the highest numbers of troops in Vietnam at nearly 540,000. Nixon was like his predecessor as he wanted peace but he too didn't want to be the first president to lose a war. The Republicans had been strong opponents to the spread of communism and he feared he would be considered weak if he simply withdrew.

However, by March 1969 the number of dead soldiers in Vietnam surpassed those that died in battle in Korea with no end in sight. The war was costing the U.S. government more than $2 billion a month, causing inflation and threatening the stability of the economy.

The NVA and the VC used Cambodia as a launching area against South Vietnam. The enemies were well entrenched in the countryside and used these boundaries to attack different military installations from their base camps.

Nixon was frustrated and ordered "secret" bombings of Cambodia with the approval of Cambodia's leader, who stood against the North Vietnamese. These secret missions by the U.S. into Laos and Cambodia were to disrupt the offensive tactics of the NVA. The U.S. began their campaign on March 18, 1969, with more than 3,600 flights dropping over 2.7 million tons of bombs in the next fourteen months, more than dropped during WWII.

The Secretary of Defense Mel Laird coined the phrase "Vietnamization" whereby the U.S. would upgrade the ARVN troops from World War II and Korean War surplus weapons to the M-16 rifle. We'd provide the supplies, weapons, ammunition and vehicles along with additional training for their Air Force and armored units. The South Vietnamese would provide the manpower for fighting. This strategy was widely broadcast and resulted in favorable ratings for Nixon.

An event occurred during 1969 that forced Nixon and the military to alter their strategy in Vietnam. This battle became known as "Hamburger Hill." The A Shau Valley had always been a stronghold of the NVA and a storage point for weapons and supplies off the Ho Chi Minh Trail.

Ten U.S. battalions were supported by artillery and air ships to secure Hill 937, a small mountain top near Laos in northwest South Vietnam. NVA soldiers were waiting in bunkers, tunnels, trenches, spider holes and fortified command posts.

This assault by the 101st Airborne and ARVN forces began on May 10, 1969 and cost 350 lives before they overtook it on May 20. When the soldiers stood on the top of the hill, a soldier inscribed in a charred tree stump, "Hamburger Hill." Beneath it, another soldier wrote, "Was it worth it?" However, by June 5th, the Army command ordered it abandoned.

The U.S. politicians and the general population questioned such useless and wasteful tactics in the war effort. Based on these negative news reports, Nixon announced that he was reducing the number of Americans serving in Vietnam. By mid-1969, 25,000 troops left, and another 85,000 were out by the end of the year. He further stated that all troops would be out of Vietnam by 1970 or 1971 at the latest. The military wanted to, (ordered to) withdraw from these battles and focus on retaining current territories.

The Paris Peace Talks officially began on May 20, 1969 but soon it was clear that negotiations were not producing any results. "Secret" negotiations directly between the U.S. and North Vietnamese began, eliminating the Viet Cong and South Vietnamese.

Kissinger began his diplomatic missions in Paris to come up with a solution. The North was reluctant to give in as they knew the U.S. was pulling its troops so they played the waiting game. Although Ho Chi Minh had died on September 3, 1969, his successor, Pham Van Dong followed the same principles of total Vietnam sovereignty.

The bombing strategy was to provide time for the ARVN to assume a greater role in the war and provide cover for U.S. troop withdrawals from Vietnam. The North continued its pressure and attacks. Nixon was upset that the North would not negotiate a reasonable settlement that would allow the U.S. to exit Vietnam and achieve "peace with honor." Nixon and Kissinger vowed that they would "bomb North Vietnam back into the stone age."

We were not seeing much action on a local level. Nixon was committed to bringing home more troops, and we questioned how long we would remain there and who would protect us.

I was scheduled to leave Vietnam in March of 1970 as my tour was near the end. I had received orders for Ft. Collins in Colorado for the remaining year of my commitment. I had an option to extend my stay in Vietnam with some perks. There were few inspections, whereas they occurred weekly stateside. I'd get a free thirty-day leave back home, another R&R, combat pay and tax free income. And, my brother could have avoided a transfer to Nam.

I didn't expect much change in the coming months, so I made a decision to re-up for another six months and return to Vietnam after taking a thirty day leave home. Unknown to me at the time, Don was already in Vietnam and participating in his own war.

Army Commendation Medal
Colonel, Mark, CW2 Ives

Part Two

Don Shaughnessy

Chapter Four

Don's Early Years

Born on July 20, 1949, I was the last child in a family of three brothers and a sister. My mother Louise raised me from birth due to my father's illness and premature death. At about the same time, we moved from the Edgewood district to the Harbor area which remains home to my family to this day.

I was born into our family that lived in a boxcar on the south ridge of town. I didn't know much about it until fifth grade when I was doing a report on Abe Lincoln. My brothers and I were sitting around the bedroom and I said that Abe was born in a log cabin. My brother Pat said to me, "No shit, what else did they have back then?" Then he told me to go to school and ask my buddies how many of them were born in a boxcar. I am sure it was the same number as those that were born in a log cabin but I wasn't going to ask.

I worked in the neighborhood during the summers mowing lawns to earn some money. Gasoline was about twenty-five cents a gallon at the time, so it cost me less than five cents to fill up my mower. At our corner gas station on 9th and Lake Avenue, I was pouring gas in my mower and noticed a little extra would trickle out from the hoses. To save five cents, I drained all the gas in the hoses, enough to fill up my lawnmower. The owner, Stanley Giddings, would yell that I owed him money, but I would point to the price on the pump that showed zero. To this day, he still kids me that I stole gas from him.

I attended Mother of Sorrows elementary and grade school through eighth grade. We were Irish Catholics and my mother scraped up the money so we could attend our local parish school. That was quite a feat for my mom, especially with five kids and no husband. The church is still there but the elementary school has closed like many other Catholic schools across the nation.

Being a young Catholic also meant being a good salesman. We sold magazines, wrapping paper, candy and just about anything to make money for the church. They had monthly raffles for $1,000, held a summer fair that my brother Jim sometimes managed, and numerous other fund raising events. Anything for a buck.

My mother cleaned houses and took in laundry to make ends meet. Before I was in school, my mother took me on a bus uptown; walked across the Spring St. Bridge, then cleaned a house while I sat on the kitchen floor. Then we walked back across the bridge and took a bus home. When I started school, she got a job during the day. Later, she worked for many years at Molded Fiber Glass. Although working in fiberglass was tough on some people, she enjoyed her job and her fellow workers.

Many of the grade school teachers were nuns at Mother of Sorrows. Although these women didn't have children, they were in charge of a bunch of kids. I believe they meant well, but they were tough to deal with. They would yell, hit kids with a ruler, and sometimes they even got mean.

When I was drafted into the Army, the Drill Sergeants screamed and yelled at us to break us down. A small, black drill sergeant came over to me and said, "Shaughnessy, this screaming and yelling doesn't seem to bother you that much." I told him I went to Catholic school. He laughed and said that this was going to be a piece of cake for me.

We lived at 823 Lake Avenue growing up, a great old fashioned neighborhood with lots of houses. Now, the area is an auto dealer lot, a take out store and a small office building. Then, we lived across the street from a coal company and Laird Lumber company.

The lumber yard gave me and my friends Chuck and John McEndree a lot of entertainment, from playing in the sawdust to hiding between boards of lumber. It also provided scraps for tree houses and weapons for sword fights. Behind the lumber yard were train tracks and I occasionally hopped a train, taking me far beyond where I knew where I was. And then, I had to walk back.

The coal yard provided our family with heat in the winter as our furnace was coal driven. When I was about eight, my mother told me that my summer job was to pick up bits of coal from the railroad tracks and fill the coal bin in our basement. I used my little red wagon to carry the coal and soon determined that it was going to take a lot longer than the summer to fill up the coal bin. My mother was very religious and would never suggest I take coal from the coal company, but I wasn't as devout as she was. I used my wagon to get some larger pieces from the edges of the coal piles, and I completed my task by early summer.

In eighth grade, a great day happened when we installed a gas converter unit in our furnace, and this meant a warm house. Plus, we no longer had to take the cinders, or clinkers, out for the trash man to collect. However, in the winter, we used those cinders to help us get our car unstuck, so it was a mixed blessing.

I went to school from kindergarten through high school with my first best friend Lenny Peaspanen. I was about half Lenny's size, but when he went out for football, I did too. In seventh grade, Lenny and I went to Dr. Macauley to get our physicals to play football. He looked at both of us and said that I could play, but I had to stay out of Lenny's way. I started at right guard on offense and defense. Lenny was the right end. He was too big for the backfield because there was a weight limit for running backs.

In 1963, I went to Harbor High School along with many of my friends. I played football in ninth grade but I was so small and slow. I didn't think the coach wanted to waste his time on me. I weighed less than 100 pounds and was usually one of the smallest in my class until late in high school. Being on the team was fun and it taught me lessons; the main one being that I wasn't a football player.

The sports I played were pickup games. We played baseball up the street at the school yard, basketball at the local YMCA, and whiffle ball in the backyard. Nothing tasted better than a drink of cold water after playing ball. It was a great life.

All of the Shaughnessy kids had jobs. My oldest brother Jim went to work at R.W. Sidley driving a cement truck when he was only 15 years old. My brother Pat followed Jim to Sidleys a few years later. Mark caddied and eventually became the caddy master, a job equivalent to a rock star back then.

During my high school years, I worked at the Ashtabula Country Club (ACC) doing odd jobs in the clubhouse from setting up for banquets and washing dishes to caddying in the summers. When I started caddying, I was so small that I could only carry one bag at a time. If I could carry two bags, I could double my pay. The ACC is one of those classic old golf courses that wasn't very long but it was hilly. The disadvantage to caddying for two golfers was that the course was very challenging with water or woods on virtually all the holes. With two guys hitting it all over, we had to watch the ball very closely in order to find it.

The following year I grew a little and was able to handle a "double eighteen." While walking up the steep hill from hole number two to number three carrying those old leather bags with thin leather straps cutting into my shoulders, I thought that there is no way I would make the full round. But I did, and got paid about $5-$6 a round. Occasionally, I caddied eighteen holes in the morning, another eighteen in the afternoon and nine more at night.

I had a great time caddying and had lots of laughs. I'm a big fan of the movie *Caddyshack*, as is just about anybody who caddied. Caddying was a great life experience. I met a lot of guys who I am still friends with today; Joe, Jake and Jim Rose, Monte Foltz, Mark and Chuck Andrews and many others. We still laugh about those times. A lot of the members were great to caddy for, but we had fun even with the ones who weren't so nice. Jake Rose and I still play golf at the same course, but there are no longer any caddies. They would be laughing at our lack of ability just like we did to those we caddied for.

I developed a strong relationship with the manager of the country club, Norman Gilbert, known as just Gil, which would be beneficial a few years later. He was a great guy who enjoyed his free time and created a positive working atmosphere at the club. He put on great luncheons for Mother's Day and other special occasions.

One night, after closing the Spot Café on Fifth Street, a couple guys and I were all heading to my cottage located behind Lou's Stagecoach, a great restaurant that served the best steaks in town. Dale Theis (DT) and I were in my big Ford Galaxy. I had taken the back seat out of the car because, at an earlier party at my cottage, there weren't enough seats for everyone. I improvised then by replacing the back seat with lawn chairs and everyone had a laugh riding in them. We had been drinking so nobody wanted to ride in the very mobile lawn chairs.

I had far too much to drink and the next thing I know I was stuck in the bushes in front of the Ashtabula Country Club. I had wiped out about twenty feet of hedges and the guys stopped to help push it out, but we couldn't budge the car. Somebody called a wrecker and everybody took off because we knew the next person coming was the Highway Patrol.

Upon arrival, the cop asked me to help him measure the damage to the bushes. I held one end of the tape measure but, as he walked to the other end, I fell into the bushes. He accurately figured I was drunk. He had me do the routine of spreading my legs a little, putting my head back and touching my nose. I missed. I lied and told him that I'm left handed and he let me try again. I spread my arms out and instead of touching my nose I just grabbed my entire face then maneuvered my finger to the nose.

Thank god he got a good laugh out of it. He called Gil, the manager of the club, and although I hadn't seen him in years, he bailed me out and didn't press charges. Of course, my friends referred to me as "the landscaper" for awhile.

I also lived with my brother Mark at the ACC, and although there were massive quantities of beer, we rarely abused the privilege. We were living there because the insurance company wanted someone to keep people from breaking in and stealing the beer, as it was readily available in the cooler. Since we knew the perpetrators, we often had them stop in for a couple beers. Mark didn't drink beer, but I did, but not enough to notice. We ate well; often starting with a dozen shrimp coupled with a steak and baked potato.

Joe Vetrano and I went to Harbor High School together. Joe, John Pokky, Don Schoendorfer and John Rapose (drafted a month earlier than me) ate lunch at my house during our senior year and we watched Jeopardy every day. I lived just a few blocks from school and it was a good break in the day. Occasionally, on weekends, we got quarts of beer and listened to music while solving the world's problems. There was a lot of good music at that time--Dylan, Doors, Stones, Cream, and Hendrix, among many other great bands.

During the summer of 1967, the year I graduated from high school, a few of us from high school began playing softball every day and then we'd have a few beers. On weekends, we went to Geneva-on-the-Lake and listened to some good rock and roll. Beer always made the music sound better. It was a great summer and marked the beginning of the Gashouse Gang. We played softball for years and continued to have an occasional beer.

The Gashouse Gang consisted of Jim Lambros, Al Sidbeck. John Pokky, Dennis Fusco, Bob Sholtis, Dave "Mutty" Ruuska, Frank Enricco, Joe Vetrano, Dennis McKenzie, Pat Donahoe, Craig Myllymaki, John Konegni, Ken Malin, Al Goodwin and a 'Bula' guy Corky Norton. There were about twenty of us. We held numerous parties, joined a softball league and are still represented today at the less strenuous game of bocci in league play. They are some of my best friends and are always good for a lot of laughs when we get together.

The infamous annual Fourth of July party started with the Gashouse Gang sitting around my house cooking burgers on a small grill and enjoying a keg of beer. A few traditions started then. Dick "Ridiculous" Daniels would always lay under the keg with the tap on and Jimmy Lambros always threw the empty keg.

In later years, this party grew to hundreds of guests with beer trucks dispensing a record nineteen kegs. I rented four Port-O-Lets so my bathroom would continue to function and to provide convenience for a lot of people drinking a lot of beer. I had certain rules for the party. The guys were to donate cash for the beer, and the women were supposed to bring the food. The rule was if you didn't bring food you had to sleep with me. We always had way too much food!

We played volleyball and bocci and ate meat on a spit. Elliot Godleski, Chris Saverise, Larry Mozzocco, and Spanky Carano prepared the meat and it was the highlight of the day. Over time, the party got out of control. When people came up to me and asked who I was, coupled with a warning from a lawyer friend of the potential liability from all the drinking, I shut it down.

I signed up for classes at the Ashtabula campus of Kent State University. I went since my friends Jimmy, Sid, and John Pokky started their college careers there. I wasn't into it as much as I should have been and had a disappointing first year. I also worked at Smith Auto Parts as a delivery man and counter salesman even though I knew nothing about cars. With the manuals in front of me, I got by.

In early 1968, the Vietnam War was really hot and heavy. The deadliest day of the war was January 31, 1968 when 246 died, many from the battle of Khe Sanh during the Tet offensive. The peak fatality month of the war was February 1968 when 3,895 soldiers died. The war started hitting home with the deaths of Fred Theis, Dale's older brother, Dave Licate, Greg Mossford and Jerry Alferink. By the end of the war, we had lost nearly thirty guys from Ashtabula County.

Mark was drafted in March 1968. Serving in the military was common in the family. My brother Jim was drafted in the late 1950s. He was stationed in Hawaii when he got orders and flew about eight hours to Vietnam, but they turned around and aborted the mission. Marge, the second oldest, married George Branscome, a cook in the Army. Brother Pat was 4-F, not eligible to serve, mainly due to poor eyesight.

During that time, there was a great deal of unrest, not only on college campuses, but also at the 1968 Democratic Convention where a groundswell of anger resulted in Richard Nixon becoming president after declaring he had a solution to the Vietnam War.

Although I was draft eligible, I was hoping that the negotiations between the U.S. and the North Vietnamese would end the war prior to my being part of it. I got drafted within three days of exactly a year after my brother, in March of 1969, while he was heading to Vietnam. The future was uncertain, and I would have to wait to see how it would impact me. While the war was unpopular with students, the general public supported it, but my friends and I thought little about it.

When I was drafted, I was just an average guy who never touched weapons or hunted. Hunting was common in parts of Ohio where I grew up. Many are drawn toward these outdoor activities, but not me. I was a city boy. While this was often passed down through generations, there was nobody left to pass it along as my father and grandfather died when I was a child.

We played army and cowboys and Indians, but I didn't have any experience with hunting or fishing. Anything that I have ever done outdoors was taught to me by the Army, except for a couple years in the Boy Scouts. I was uninterested in guns and remain so today. Not that there's anything wrong with it. There was nothing in my background that would suggest I should be in the infantry.

I had a small taste of war, and it didn't taste very good. I was in the early stages of Operation Ripcord, one of the last great battles of the Vietnam War. I was there in some fierce battles for a few short months but I won't pretend to be an expert on Vietnam or the war. However, I had a ring-side seat to some tense moments and heroic actions from the guys around me.

I know it's hard for people to relate to the experience of war or to fully describe it, but this is my attempt at explaining it. My memories of the war often come to me in random fashion, so if I skip around a little, pretend we are in a bar and you are sitting next to me as I ramble along. By the way, it's your turn to buy.

Chapter Five

Don Drafted

The draft loomed large on the horizon, and when I received my draft notice to report on March 9, 1969, along with friends Vince Degennaro and Dennis Fusco, I fully accepted it and prepared for my physical. I kissed my mother goodbye, and told her not to worry. Looking back, the person who really took it on the chin was my mother Louise. One son was already in Vietnam and now I was drafted. I can only imagine how she worried, so when I wrote her, I tried to make it a fun read.

Dennis Fusco and his father picked me up. Our friend Al Sidbeck rode with us uptown to an uncertain future. I put on the Doors "Unknown Soldier" and left the house with that song blaring. We went to the Red Cross building on Center Street where they gave us a Bible, an apple and some shaving gear. I had a nowhere job and I wasn't very good in school. I went into the Army with the philosophy of Bob Dylan, "When you ain't got nothing, you got nothing to lose."

On 10 March 1969, I was officially sworn in as a member of the U.S. Army and shipped to Ft. Campbell, Kentucky for basic training. Ft. Campbell was home of the 101st Airborne division and already a large contingent of our Vietnam fighting force. As part of the initiation, we were offered opportunities to elect a MOS, or job, but only if we extended our time in the Army for an additional year. After I took a number of tests, they recommended I work in finance or become a Warrant Officer and helicopter pilot. But that was a six-year commitment, and would likely include a tour in Vietnam.

The lieutenant in charge recommended finance but said they really needed riflemen. That should have been a tip off that if I didn't choose my MOS, they would choose it for me, and that was likely going to be the infantry.

Getting drafted was probably a good thing for me. Physically, it was tough, but I had been playing a lot of pickup basketball so the exercise part wasn't as difficult as it was on others. Mentally, at nineteen, they could mold me into anything they wanted, and they did.

The first days in the Army were hectic. I had long hair close to the shoulder, but not for long. At my first haircut, we lined up and the barber was hustling us through. When I sat in his chair he asked me if I wanted my curl in front and I said "yes sir" and he said "catch it." I was laughing while he shaved my head. We had to pay 75 cents for that haircut and it was taken out of our monthly check which, by the way, was only $97 a month.

The barracks we were going to live in for the next nine weeks were old. We had a bed and a foot locker that had to be ready for inspection at all times, so we put everything in order on top-- shaving gear, toothbrush, and towels.

The first night I took a late shower and, after we went to bed, guys were talking to no one in particular and complaining about their bed, which was a set of bunk beds, with a nice thick mattress. When I was living at home in an upstairs apartment with my mother and brother Pat, I had to sleep on a studio couch that always left me with a stiff neck--that kind of stiff neck that when somebody behind you yells your name, you turn your whole body like Igor. It was lights out at 10 p.m. or 2200 for you civilians. I lay in that nice comfortable bed and thought, so far so good.

The fifty guys in our platoon were from all over the country and, everybody got along. The drill sergeants were on us a lot and I remember running and doing pushups all the time. To get control of the troops, they identified the biggest or toughest guy and rode him hard so everybody knew who was in charge.

All and all, the drill sergeants, also called drill instructors, or DIs, were pretty good guys. The difficulty in pronouncing my name became both a negative and a positive. Early on, as the drill sergeant was studying my name, I volunteered by pronouncing it correctly, and he snapped back, "I know how to pronounce your name, do you think I'm stupid?" He gave me fifty pushups. After that, I never volunteered my name or much of anything else. In some instances, I could see the sergeants looking over names for duty and would pass on mine, giving the jobs to Smith and Thompson instead. Some duty included K-P, or Kitchen Police, which meant we cleaned up the kitchen, washed dishes, cleaned the floors, and prepared the "mess hall" for the next meal.

Basic training was getting people in shape and largely consisted of us running everywhere. We were up everyday around 5:30 a.m. (0530) and started out running a mile. By the end of basic, we were easily doing three miles in combat boots. In fact, in the last week of training, we could opt out of running but we still did it because it felt good. After the run, it was back to the barracks. The guys with heavy beards had to shave. I was one of the fair haired guys so, to prevent a log jam in the morning, we shaved at night.

Then off to the chow line. Everything you heard about Army food is true. It was tasteless, but it kept us going. I went in weighing 140 pounds and came out of eight weeks of basic at about 165 pounds because of pushups, running and eating everything I could find. I got to know a lot of guys in the platoon because I was so hungry. I sat by the exit of the mess hall and when guys left with leftover food, I would ask for it. A couple black guys from the South couldn't believe I'd eat their food. Remember, this was the sixties, and we were in the South.

Another part of basic training is orienting to the Army. That included teaching us how to salute, handle a weapon, shoot on the range, prepare for inspections, pack so everything fits in one duffle bag and roll clothes so they would not wrinkle while traveling. This was an important part of travel that would come in handy in the future.

The first time we went to the rifle range to shoot the M-14, we were there all day and we only shot three bullets. They stressed safety and they had to. The instructors walked everyone through the steps, but some guys couldn't follow instructions.

Anyone who has been in the service remembers hearing, "Ready on the left, Ready on the right," followed with "Commence fire, commence fire." Then the bullets would fly for about 20 seconds and then we heard, "Cease fire, cease fire." That was always followed with a couple stray sounds of gunfire. The DI went to the guy and hit him on the head. Of course, the guy turned around and pointed his rifle at the drill sergeant. It was comical.

Vince "Dege" Degennaro was in my company but, since the platoons were sorted in alphabetical order, he was in first platoon and I was in fourth platoon. Vince and I had gone to school from kindergarten through high school together. He had a great sense of humor and that helped a lot. It was uplifting seeing him from time to time. Many times we couldn't talk but I could see his grin and I knew that he was thinking, "What a crock of shit."

Dennis "Spic" Fusco was drafted the same day as me, but went to another company so I very seldom saw him. He became a company cook and stayed at Ft. Campbell. A few years after we got back, we talked about our experiences and he told me how he wanted to go to Vietnam, but his commanding officer wouldn't let him go. When you have a dedicated worker like Dennis, you don't let him go. Eventually he and Dege went to Germany.

Although the weather was relatively mild for the eight weeks from mid-March to mid-May, it became hotter in Kentucky as my training continued. And, as my training advanced, the weather would only get worse.

Basic training was a good experience. Near its completion, I was uncertain about my future as I had not received my orders for AIT, Advanced Individual Training. Finally, I received them and it was for Infantry, the dreaded 11 Bravo MOS, and off to even warmer temperatures in Louisiana.

Advanced Individual Training

After completing basic, I was sent on a fourteen-hour bus ride to Ft. Polk, Louisiana, my home for the next nine weeks for Advanced (Infantry) Training. I learned real quick that it gets much hotter in the South and much earlier than northeast Ohio.

We arrived in the rain and were ushered into very old WWII barracks with no air conditioning about 2 a.m. The drill sergeant introduced himself. He said that Ft. Polk was the home of infantrymen and that we were going to Vietnam. Further, he said that ninety-nine percent of us would go to Vietnam and the other one percent would die there during training. I was beginning to wonder what I got myself into.

No, our drill sergeant wasn't named Sergeant Hulka and he wasn't the big toe from the movie *Stripes*, but he was close. The training at Ft. Polk was intense as the weather conditions somewhat mirrored Vietnam. It lived up to its name, "Tigerland." It was hot and muggy and after it rained it was steamy hot, nearly unbearable. We marched everywhere and sang, "I want to go to Vietnam, I want to kill a Viet Cong."

In basic training, we used the M-14 rifle, but at Ft. Polk, we were introduced to the new and controversial M-16 rifle. After seeing it, I asked the sergeant when we were getting the real rifle. It was plastic and small compared to the M-14, and light at about six pounds. It looked like Mattel made it, but he assured me it was the real thing. It wasn't as accurate as the M-14 but it could put out the firepower, up to a 1,000 rounds a minute. They slowed it down a little to around 700-900 rounds a minute to keep it from jamming.

During the first M-16 demonstration, the sergeant put the rifle on his crotch and pulled the trigger, shooting twenty rounds to show how little kick there was to the weapon. Of course, we later kidded that he sang soprano in the church choir. We carried this weapon every day and cleaned it every night. The Army believed in repetition as a learning technique. I think to this day I could take one apart and put it together.

We learned about different weapons and military maneuvers. We fired the M-60 machine gun, something we relied on in Vietnam. We threw grenades. We shot a .50 caliber antiaircraft weapon--just two rounds would take a telephone pole down.

First aid training was emphasized because we might be the only one around to help someone. We waded through water pits and looked for weapons in a fake village. The classrooms were either out in the field or in buildings around the base. We slept in the barracks at night, but one week we bivouacked out in the field on Peason Ridge to simulate Vietnam. We dug bunkers and filled sand bags. The weather was hot, so they got that part right. The training was good, but it really should have been longer.

We liked our company first sergeant. He had been to Vietnam and we wanted him to command us over there. He said that if he took us over he'd make sure we came home one way or another, dead or alive. I guess that was good to hear. Any time we made a mistake like running upright instead of crawling, or making too much noise, he would say that if we made that mistake in Vietnam, "One year from that day, you will have been dead one year." I really didn't know if I was ready for Nam but, as the end of AIT got closer, I made up my mind that I wasn't going to worry and just do the best I could.

Many combat troops were given nominal training, just basic training and advanced infantry training before being sent to Vietnam. I was about to receive even more advanced training, yet the Vietnam experience was still overwhelming.

The company commander was catching flak for not sending enough guys to Non-Commissioned Officers (NCOC) School. He applied pressure to each soldier who qualified for NCO school by having them do pushups in the heat until they volunteered to attend. He met his quota. Thirty other guys and I "volunteered" for twelve weeks of NCOC School at Ft. Benning, Georgia. In addition, an additional nine weeks of training other soldiers made up the entire twenty-one week program. The program was initially begun for the infantry but soon expanded to other combat arms such as mortars, etc.

We were considered "Shake n' Bake," as we received intensive training and promotions in a short period of time. I had mixed emotions. We would be promoted from Private First Class (PFC) to Sergeant, up two pay grades. Instead of listening to orders, we would be giving them as squad leaders and eventually platoon sergeants. The rub against these NCOs was that some of them were jerks. There is nothing worse than a prick with a little bit of power. I was going to Ft. Benning and tell them I wanted to drop out. But first, I was taking leave for a few weeks back in Ashtabula.

It was nice getting home, especially in the summer. The Gashouse Gang played softball and I got to sit back and have a few beers. Even though I was in the Army, we talked sparingly about Vietnam and just enjoyed the moment. It was nice seeing Lenny, Jimmy, Sid, Mutty and the rest of the guys.

During that summer of 1969, the "Sixties Generation" was being remembered more for the celebration of four days of Woodstock, where more than 400,000 kids played in the mud at the famed rock concert. About 8,500 miles away, another 400,000 soldiers were fighting in Vietnam and during those same four days, 109 soldiers died.

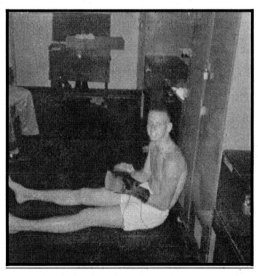

Don-Shining shoes in basic training

Entrance to Ft. Polk

Peason Ridge-Ft. Polk Building a bunker

Fort Benning, Georgia-NCOC School

The NCO school for non-commissioned officers was held at Ft. Benning, Georgia, about ten miles from Columbus, located in the middle and western part of the state, bordering Alabama.

By the third year of the war in Vietnam, the Army was running short of qualified leaders. West Point graduates made up less than five percent of the total and ROTC membership had dwindled with the active protests against the military. Some "lifers" in the military started to question the war and senior NCOs took retirement at twenty years instead of the thirty-year milestone. This shortage led to recruiting those with leadership potential to attend the rigorous twenty-one-week NCO school.

The school started in 1967. One of the men responsible for this program was Lt. Col. David Hackworth. We trained for twelve weeks and if we graduated, we went to Phase 1 (OJT) on the job training. We were assigned to serve as platoon sergeants at a military post stateside to oversee training of troops with the same MOS (Military Occupational Specialty). Phase 2 took place in Vietnam or Korea where we continued our responsibilities as platoon sergeants or squad leaders.

The idea was revolutionary and controversial from the start. Many older NCOs had difficulty giving rapid advancement to men new to the military when it took them years of hard work to make rank. The challenges of Vietnam made the Army break with the outdated, past practices. Unlike Korea or WWll, Vietnam was not a senior commander war, that is, a war covering large areas of terrain. Rather, this was a jungle war with small areas of operation and the brunt of the fighting fell on the junior officers and NCOs.

Upon arrival, I wanted to get out of NCO school as I felt I was coerced into signing up. However, my commander said that it would be better if I stayed--I could either command others, or they would command me. He pointed to a few soldiers that were not very good, and he said that I was going to have to take orders from these guys over in Vietnam if I bailed out of the program. I reluctantly stayed.

The curriculum consisted of more in-depth training on weapons like the M-16, M-60 and grenades, plus the art of combat. Also, first aid, radio training, explosives, and map reading were important parts of the program. We had classroom work and then went out in the field to apply the principles.

Many who entered the NCO program did not graduate and a certain percent were dropped each week. Weekly tests and results from field activities determined our skill level and whether we continued through the program. Situation training, where we were thrown into battle challenges, was particularly rewarding, as we knew it would help us stay alive once we encountered the enemy. Some of the training was copied from Nazi Germany officer training. We knew we were headed to Vietnam, and we wanted to be fully prepared to survive our future. The atmosphere was very gung-ho at Ft. Benning, but we were somewhat guarded.

On September 3, 1969, our company of about 200 listened as the instructor said he had good news. He announced that Ho Chi Minh, the leader of North Vietnam, had just died. His announcement was met with dead silence. I sensed that he and the other officers in the room expected a big cheer, but it wasn't happening. We felt that Ho didn't do anything to us, so just train us well and let us go do it. More than 20,000 graduated from the school from 67-72 and over 1,000 were killed in Vietnam.

The success of the program is debatable as the training was good, but we were unsure who we would be leading. The concept was not thought out well as we had no interaction with those we would command. We were getting advanced training while other "grunts" were going to Vietnam with only basic and AIT training.

As training ended, we selected Ft. Polk to spend our next nine weeks training other soldiers stateside. Tim Palmer, a friend of mine from Anoka, Minnesota, and I took off for Ft. Polk, about a twelve-hour trip, and we picked up Ben Simon from Louisiana on the way. The three of us ended up in the same company, training new soldiers. *I've talked to Tim off and on since the war. We had a lot of laughs in the Army and it was guys like him and Ben that made it a good experience.*

Fort Polk-Again

Upon completion of the NCO program, I went back to Ft. Polk for a nine-week period to train other troops. During that time, I met Dick Huhta, a high school classmate of my brother Mark. Dick had recently returned from Vietnam and he was also training troops. He added credibility as he spent more than a year in combat near Saigon in the southern part of Vietnam. He cautioned me not to go to Vietnam unless I had to. Since Mark was there, I didn't have to go. The Army had a rule from World War II that more than one brother doesn't have to be in a war zone at the same time, as featured in the movie *Saving Private Ryan*.

However, I felt a strong allegiance toward those I trained with and wanted to be part of a unit that would help each other, even if it threatened my life. I was twenty and felt this was just another challenge and I was going to let the chips fall where they may. How often do you get a chance to go to war? I got caught up in all the B.S.

Overall, my training was extensive, consisting of ten months of learning about infantry, plus a couple weeks of leave, adding up to nearly a full year before I received my orders for Vietnam. I felt ready to meet the enemy, if I needed to.

Nixon was elected based on his commitment to end the Vietnam War. He had been in office nearly a year and we thought that the war was going to wind down at any time. We had seen the start of troop reduction in 1969 and an additional 80,000 or so were out by year-end, and he promised further reductions. One instructor at Ft. Benning said the war might be over before we got there, but he was wrong. The negotiators argued for months about the shape of the negotiating table, so my hopes for averting time in Vietnam were low.

I received my orders for Vietnam in January 1970, and would depart soon after I took a two-week leave in Ashtabula. Also, I visited Jimmy Lambros and Al Sidbeck at Kent State, John Pokky at Ohio State, as well as Joe Vetrano and Bob Sholtis at Ohio University where my brother Jim had attended.

I knew I was doing something momentous, but it just didn't click. I knew Joe, Jim and Sid were really more upset about me going to Vietnam than I was. I also spent time with those remaining in Ashtabula unaffected by the draft, drinking beer and hanging out, not thinking about the future. After reading the history of those times, one would think that everyone was protesting the war but, in reality, life went on.

Although Nixon ended the draft, protesting against the war continued, but not as severely. Nixon was committed to ending the draft and replaced it with the lottery that began in December 1969. Birth dates were added to 366 capsules and drawn at random to determine the status of each person. The low numbers were called into service and the others remained untouched. It didn't matter to me as I was already drafted. Once the draft was banished and replaced by the lottery, protests diminished.

Some protests were aimed at ROTC on college campuses. According to a VFW article published in September 2009, in the school years 1969-70, there were more than 400 incidents against ROTC. In 1970-71, once the draft was eliminated, the number of incidences fell to about 100.

In early 1970, there were still about 425,000 troops in Vietnam. I was one of them and participated in some fierce battles that are the essence of the rest of this story.

Chapter Six

Vietnam-Don

Rather than go directly to Ft. Lewis in Washington State, I flew to Minnesota and met up with Tim Palmer, my training partner for the past several months. After a couple days in Minnesota, we set off on our journey to Vietnam. We were held in Ft. Lewis for a couple days processing. At that point, I started thinking "Holy shit, what the hell am I doing?" I was going to Vietnam with a lot of the guys I had trained with for the last six months and we were happy to see each other, but we started getting a dose of reality. You get to think a lot in an eighteen-hour flight from Ft. Lewis to Hawaii, then Guam and into Cam Ranh Bay in the southeast corner of South Vietnam.

After leaving the winter weather of Ashtabula and Minnesota, it was hot in February upon our arrival in Vietnam. We walked out of the plane door into that 100–degree-plus weather that was sucked right into our lungs. Show Time! We were shuttled by buses with chicken wire covering the windows to prevent kids from throwing rocks and grenades through the windows.

During our brief stay in Cam Ranh Bay, before going to our final destination, we spent some time in the bars that included a mixture of guys on their way home and ones arriving. We were reminded that we were guests of the South Vietnamese government and to act accordingly. We were called NFGs, New Fucking Guys, or Cherries, easily spotted since our uniforms were new and they stuck out from the worn and ragged looking ones that the "old heads," or veterans, were wearing.

There was a Vietnamese rock band playing in the bar. One of the popular songs we sang along with was the Animals hit, "We got to get out of this place." The singer sounded more like Elmer Fudd when he sang, "we got to get out of this pwace if it is the wast thwing we ever do." We all loved the band, and I still laugh when I think about it. The last song of the night was "America the Beautiful" and we sang at the top of our lungs.

These veterans, ages 21 or 22, asked me what my MOS was and I told them 11 Bravo, or infantry. They bought all of us in infantry a drink. After a couple drinks, they asked what outfits we were assigned to. I said 101st and they told me that I was going to a gung-ho unit. They motioned to the bartender that they were buying my drinks the rest of the night. I was surprised to be singled out.

They said I would get a CIB, Combat Infantry Badge, which is given to soldiers "present under hostile fire engaged in ground combat with the enemy." Okay, that is what I had been training for. Further, they said I was going to earn the Purple Heart for getting wounded. I remember drinking beer but wondering what the hell had I had gotten myself into.

But, there I was in Vietnam in early 1970. I was part of the 101st Airborne, a proud infantry unit that dated back to World War II and one of the first infantry divisions sent to Vietnam. The 101st Airborne Division, known as the "Screaming Eagles," was trained for air assault operations made famous by the book and movie *Band of Brothers*.

For historical reasons, the 101st retains the "Airborne" identity. Although some complete the Air Assault School and wear the badge, jump training is not required to be assigned to the division. I never attended jump school, and I was surprised that I was assigned to this division. I guess they just needed fresh blood. The 506th regiment of the 1st brigade was nicknamed the "Curahees" and this stems from when the regiment formed at Camp Toccoa, Georgia in 1942 and the Curahee Mountain was located inside the camp. The Cherokee word means "stand alone" and became the unit's motto.

I was assigned to Delta (D) Company of the 1st Brigade of the 506th Regiment, all under the 101st banner, thus we were D/1-506th. I received my orders and flew by a C-130 airplane to Phu Bai near Hue in the northern part of the country, close to the DMZ, or Demilitarized Zone. Hue was the hot bed of fighting since the war began, during Tet, and throughout my time in Vietnam.

Tet in 1968 was used as a springboard for a comprehensive nationwide strike against nearly all of the large cities and provincial capitals of South Vietnam.

Hue was the longest battle of the Tet offensive. One of the oldest cities in Vietnam, Hue was created in 1307 and became the center of Vietnam in 1687 and named the capital in 1778. This "old city" was home to the Citadel, a walled city that surrounds the Imperial Palace. During Tet, the VC units controlled Hue except for the MACV compound and the ARVN 1st Division.

The NVA were successful in Hue as they broke through the provincial capital, and held it for twenty-five days. There was fierce fighting, but this was an important area to control and needed to be recaptured. The Americans were able to cut off supplies and reclaim the city. Regrettably, the ancient city was left in ruins after the bombings decimated the cities infrastructure and left 115,000 civilians homeless. In the end, we had to destroy the city to save it.

After the dust settled, literally, 5,000-8,000 VC died, after they killed 2,800 Vietnamese civilians. About 150 marines from the 1st Cavalry and 101st Airborne and 400 ARVN forces lost their lives. By March, more than 58,000 Viet Cong and NVA troops were killed from the onset of the Tet offensive. The U.S. lost a total of about 2,500 and the ARVN approximately 4,000 from Tet.

The press reported the fact that a few NVA climbed inside the walls at various military encampments, including Saigon and Hue, and portrayed Tet as a victory for the North. If you simply listened to the press and read the papers, you would think the Tet offensive was our loss.

On the trip through Hue we traveled the last couple miles in the back of a deuce-and-a-half truck through this beautiful old historic city. While crossing an old bridge, I saw a big yellow and orange Shell Oil sign next to a gas station on the corner, looking out of place.

Over the next couple days, I became more accustomed to the weather. I didn't know heat until Vietnam, although our training helped somewhat. We did our best to get acclimated to such intense heat. A one week SERTS training program, or Screaming Eagles Replacement Training School, was given for all new soldiers of the 101st upon arrival in country to familiarize us to the weather, terrain and combat activities.

Vietnam was different in many ways from other wars. In *Band of Brothers,* the soldiers trained and went into battle as a well organized unit. I was expecting that those of us who trained together would be sent to Vietnam and continue to operate as one unit. Wrong again. In Vietnam, they split everyone up and sent us to units all over the country. Robert McNamara, the Secretary of Defense, thought that if soldiers became friends and someone was killed, it would devastate a unit and may lead to battle fatigue or other psychological disorders. This thinking was based on a study they did from WWII.

We were being led by the so-called "Best and the Brightest," defined in the Pulitzer Prize winning book of the same name by David Halberstam. McNamara's idea was to plug people in and if someone got killed, no one is devastated and the troops keep on going. Sometimes these separate pieces of the puzzle didn't work as a cohesive unit. Perhaps he viewed us much like an assembly line as he was the former president of Ford Motor Company.

The military learned from the mistakes of Vietnam. Today, in the Iraq War, soldiers are sent over as a unit. The members of the units get to know everyone; their strengths and weaknesses, pretty much like putting a ball team together. There is Point, Slack, and RTO just to name a few positions equivalent to a baseball team like infielders, outfielders and pitchers working together. But that wasn't how it was done then.

Going to war is obviously stressful and being sent to a unit without knowing anyone can be lonely. All the people we trained with for the past ten months were spread all over Vietnam. We developed a few close friends, so our goal becomes surviving the year, and less focused on winning the war.

Within the next few days I was going to grab an M-16 rifle, strap on some ammo and hand grenades then go put my life in the hands of complete strangers and theirs in mine. I was hoping that I didn't get stuck in right field.

All the information about peace talks and winding down the war down played in the back of our minds. This was a lot for a twenty-year-old to process. Actually, it was a lot for a number of guys, both those in the field and the NCOs and Officers leading them. I wanted to be at Ohio State trying to get laid.

There were basic terms we used to distinguish from those fighting and those in support. In the rear it was "three hots and a cot," and in the field it was "two colds and a hole." This meant the guys in the rear got three hot meals and a cot to sleep on. In the field, we got two C-rations a day and when we couldn't light a fire, we ate them cold. We dug holes in the ground for shelter, especially when the enemy mortared us.

My first night in my company I was put on CQ (Charge of Quarters) or in charge at night. The rest of the company was out in the field. This night I guarded a prisoner who had tried to "Frag," that is, he threw a grenade at and tried to kill the first sergeant, the highest ranking non-commissioned officer of the company. I just sat at a desk guarding him while he sat in a chair.

We both read or listened to the radio that was tuned to our company in the field. I had a .45 pistol to use if I needed, but I would never think of using it on another GI. The guy said he tried to kill the first sergeant and said he was going to get away and avoid going to LBJ, Long Binh Jail, located near Saigon. I told him I didn't care if he wanted to run away. He thought of himself as some type of hero. Here I am in Vietnam carrying on a conversation with a guy trying to kill one of our own. I had read Catch 22, and now I was part of it.

There is conflicting information on fragging and drug use. The majority of the fraggings and drug use were done in the rear, not in the field. There was more boredom in the rear and guys in their early twenties had greater access to cheap beer and inexpensive pot.

These temptations were not readily available in the field, and we wouldn't tolerate a guy getting high and costing us our lives. There were exceptions, notably when we went back to the rear.

I was at Camp Evans, a large base camp. It was named after Paul Evans of South Dakota, a Marine who was killed in December 1966. He was called the gentle giant because of his 6' 6" frame and his friendly nature. His fellow soldiers requested the naming of the camp in his honor. Camp Evans was like a small city that included barracks, called hootches, a PX, barber shop, NCO and EM clubs and other amenities. *According to Army Magazine, March 1998, this huge military base is now gone and the area is being farmed.*

When in the rear, we got assigned guard duty at night. The security was good with concertina wire all around the compound and minefields to protect us from sappers. Sappers were specially trained enemy soldiers who would sneak into our base camps with strapped explosives to their bodies to blow up food, fuel, ammunition, helicopters and soldiers.

There were bunkers every fifty yards and our company was responsible for manning four or five of them. Since I was a sergeant with infantry training I was put in charge, but the guys knew their job. The bunkers were manned by the troops in the rear; cooks, truck drivers, clerks, and mechanics, among others. I pulled rear guard duty a few times before going out in the field.

The second night, I had to meet with the next in command to go over the passwords. This was the first time I met Lt. Ed Deuschle my future Platoon Leader. Walking back to my position I noticed a crowd around a new guy to the company. He had shot himself in the foot with his M-16. He was a nice guy but he did not like the idea of going out in the field so he took matters into his own hands, or, in this case, his foot.

An M-16 bullet is just slightly larger than a .22 round. Usually an M-16 bullet will rip a big hole in whatever it hits. I looked at his foot and there was this small hole, a little bigger than an eraser on a pencil. It was apparent that he shot himself at point blank and it went right through his foot. He was taken to the hospital and treated.

A few days later I read over his court martial. They got him for destroying government property; listing the shoe, the sock, the shoelace, and him. His social security number was one of the items he damaged. I realized then that we were just a number.

I knew guys who desperately tried to avoid the field. One guy took a can opener and cut himself with it, saying it was a rat bite, and they had to send him to the hospital for treatment. They treated rat bites by injecting a needle in the stomach once a day for two weeks. He later said that at least he bought two more weeks of living.

For every one soldier out in the field there were about eight soldiers in support. There was a saying in the rear that "if you fuck up, you ruck up." If you didn't do your job, whether it is a clerk, truck driver, or cook, you were going to be punished by being sent out to the field to carry a rucksack and a gun.

I was going to be in the field every day so there was little that they could threaten me with. At this point, some of the infantry guys started to get the feeling that we were getting shit on, and we developed a chip on our shoulder. We used that as motivation to get ourselves pumped up for a wild ride.

I wasn't in the rear much but there were a few things I remember. We were going to a bar (Hey I'm Irish) and this young Vietnamese kid kept yelling to us, "Hey GI, momma-san cherry you want?" So we are sitting having a beer and I'm thinking that someone just offered me his mom, and she's a virgin.

During processing, our money was changed into MPCs, or Military Payment Certificates, sometimes called script. This currency was all paper, no coins or pennies, just rounded to the nearest nickel. MPCs changed occasionally, about every six months, to avert counterfeiting.

We were given about twenty-four hours to exchange it, or it became worthless. MPCs were the best currency for both Americans and Vietnamese. Their official currency was piastres, or p, but it was virtually worthless except among Vietnamese.

Giving us money when we were going out to the boonies didn't make sense. I sent most of my money home and kept a little cash to spend in case we came back to the rear. On some paydays, the first day of the month, the pay officer came out in the middle of the jungle to pay us. We were surprised but figured it was a way to boost our morale.

I thought I was ready for the field, so I loaded onto a helicopter going out to my company. Of course, if I didn't feel that I was ready, I was going anyway because those were my orders. The first chopper rides were fun during the training at Ft. Benning. Now we were with the 101st airmobile unit, and we traveled by chopper all the time. We were dropped off and picked up days or weeks later, sometimes at a different location. This ability to move troops with ease increased our exposure to combat. The average soldier in Vietnam saw 240 days of combat a year opposed to forty days in the South Pacific during WWII.

On our first ride out, the pilots would see the nice clean uniforms of a new guy and, of course, they wanted to mess with us. They'd bank the helicopter and when it tilted we thought we were going to fall out. We'd scramble to hold on, but centrifugal force wouldn't let us fall out. They got their laughs.

A few weeks later, I was riding aboard a chopper with a new uniform and the pilot did the same thing. I just sat and smiled at him and he just shrugged his shoulder as if to say, hey, I thought you were new. Thank god the pilots had the swagger that they did, as they saved many lives at great risk to themselves. *Bruce Campbell, a chopper pilot and good friend from Ashtabula, still has that cocky pilot attitude.*

The terrain dictated our ability to use certain equipment. Some units were mechanized, meaning they had tanks and APC's (Armored Personnel Carriers) that cut through the jungle. If they got ambushed they had a lot of firepower such as .50 caliber machine guns. In the flatter areas, tanks and APCs were utilized. The Navy guys down in the Mekong Delta near Saigon had boats armed with a lot of firepower. Senator John Kerry ran one of those.

Each fighting unit had their pluses and minuses. We were envious of the firepower but you couldn't sneak up on anyone with those loud machines unless you were attacking a bunch of drummers from a rock and roll band. By contrast, in the mountains, we carried our firepower; M-16s, grenades, and supplies in the rucksacks on our backs.

While flying over the terrain we saw the thick jungle and the tops of hills that had all the trees cut off. That is called a LZ, or Landing Zone. A LZ had to be at least 64 feet wide, the wing span of the helicopter blades. The LZs were all over the area, providing many places that allowed the Army to get troops in and out of almost everywhere. The jungle was so dense that it made it virtually impossible to move a large number of troops very far on land, so helicopters needed places to land and transport the troops.

Also, the jungle was the home of the Viet Cong and North Vietnamese fighting forces. They fought together for many years and won many battles simply by knowing the territory. The North Vietnamese were in the war for the duration of the war, so some of them had been fighting in these jungles for years. Unknown to us at the time, they had a well developed bunker and tunnel system as well as a reliable supply chain.

Local Bar-base camp

Huey Slick and Sgt. Fraser

Cobra Gun Ship

In the Boonies

On the first day in the field, I was taken to the top of a hill to join my company and we heard a firefight going on with another platoon not far from our location. The other platoon was at the bottom of the hill, and had made contact with the enemy. They called in gun ships, which are helicopters fitted with machine guns and grenade launchers. It was the middle of the day and we didn't go to help them because the CO said they had it under control, or so he thought.

We were told to chow down while all of this was going on. It was my first day and I wasn't that hungry. I had to be hungry to eat C-rations. Honestly, they looked and smelled like dog food. The guys on either side of me laughed and said that in a couple of days I would love the food. They were right, but at that time, I wasn't eating.

I was watching the two gun ships; one passed by and shot machine guns, and the other shot 250 twenty millimeter grenades a minute. As they made their pass, they flew right at us and stopped shooting just short of us. I said to the guys on either side of me, "Isn't that chopper getting a little close?" "Get used to it," they said. I thought that if he misses by just a little, we're dead.

They were eating and not really paying attention to the fight. Not wanting to look like a chickenshit, I put my rucksack in front of me and used it as a shield while pretending to work on the straps. About a minute later the ground started kicking up shrapnel from the grenades, from the choppers. I heard the screaming of the two guys on either side of me when they both got hit. Hot metal from the grenades hitting flesh smells like a human barbeque. Needless to say, this was an eye opener.

The pilot of the chopper that hit them hovered about twenty feet over them, and we could tell that the pilot felt real bad. The guys had to be medevaced out. They were patched up and returned to the field a few weeks later. So, there I was in the field just a couple of hours and two guys were down from friendly fire.

After the gun ships took out the enemy, a couple of guys from the other platoon went to check on the dead enemy soldiers. As they rolled one of them over, the guy was still alive and had a live grenade. The last thing he did in his life was kill two more Americans. My baptism under fire was a learning experience all the way around; watch out for stray rounds from our gun ships, and make sure the dead are really dead. I was starting to see what the guys in the bar were telling me. We had to be mindful about any danger, either from the enemy or our own. I was apprehensive about facing a year of this activity.

Each unit had to have a point man and a slack man. Point walked first and a point man's life expectancy was less than a second in a firefight. The slack man walked next, about five or ten feet behind and that bought him a couple more seconds of life.

Next were the squad leader and his RTO (Radio Telephone Operator). We all stayed about ten yards from each other so if a bomb, mortar or grenade went off it would only injure one or two guys rather than everyone. We all heard during training that we should spread out or, "One round will get you all."

The rest of the squad filled in after the RTO. When I first got out there I was not a squad leader. I walked near rear security with other new guys, right in front of the guy in rear security to gather as much information from him as I could absorb. Melvin Hollingsworth (Holly) was usually the guy in the back as he had a habit of always looking over his shoulder so he was the perfect guy for that job. We didn't want anyone sneaking up on us. Of course, when attacked and the proverbial shit hit the fan, things changed. I always thought of firefights as organized confusion.

I went over as a sergeant, a so called shake n' bake and I didn't know how I would be welcomed. Some new sergeants were resented as they had the title but no real war experience to back it up and sometimes put their men in harm's way. I was warmly received as just another guy with a rifle in the unit. I asked a lot of questions and tried to fit into the team and take on all tasks. In a group of about twenty-five guys 24/7, I learned to adapt.

One of the first jobs I did was to stand on the LZ and direct a chopper coming in for a landing. I stood with the wind either at my back or facing it, ensuring that it was not blowing to my left or right. When the wind blew side to side, it was difficult for the chopper to land. We popped smoke and held up our arms level and when the slick hits the ground, we cross our arms to signify to the pilot that he has touched ground.

I was more than six feet tall so when I raised my arms, the chopper blades were just barely above me. I had visions of the blades slicing off my arms. After a couple times, I got down on my knees to provide me a little more space and less stress on my mind. Plus, I realized that I was standing out in the open on the LZ, a prime target for a sniper to pick me off. I knew I was thin, but I wasn't that skinny.

The mountains surrounding us were a challenge and would remain that way over the ensuing months. We went up and down the mountains carrying a heavy rucksack. The wet jungle and the steep terrain made for slippery footing and difficult maneuvering. Sometimes, we gained control of the top of the mountain and stayed there to protect it. Other times, we secured a mountain top, but were pulled off it to fight the enemy elsewhere, and had to regain it later. This wasn't a battle about taking territory like previous wars; this was about killing the enemy.

The theory was if you went in high terrain, you stayed high, but if you went in low, you stayed low. This didn't always work, but that was the strategy. It wasn't easy to keep control of our position as the enemy also saw the benefits of mountain top superiority. However, being on top allowed the enemy to zero in on it as a target and would shoot mortars in throughout the day and night coupled with the threat of sapper attacks at night.

In other instances, we went in low to fight the enemy at jungle level. Much of our fighting occurred down there with brush too thick to move. The fear of booby traps weighed heavily on our minds. We couldn't see far in front of us and an enemy ambush was a constant threat. They could strike and then retreat into their tunnels.

The North Vietnamese became famous for building an infrastructure of tunnels whereby they moved their fighters from one location to another without going through the thick brush. The tunnels consisted of sleeping quarters and contained food, supplies, ammunition and even hospital units to care for their wounded.

Although these tunnels were difficult to locate, they were even harder to penetrate. Since the average Vietnamese man weighed less than a hundred pounds, they could travel through the tunnels with ease whereas a GI would struggle fitting in them.

The smallest guy in the unit was the tunnel rat and was called upon to check out the tunnels, sometimes with fatal results. They could encounter the enemy, be bitten by snakes or die from suffocation. In my squad we never used a tunnel rat. Some used them more than others. We had a few short guys that probably fit, but I could never order someone into a tunnel.

I did many things in Vietnam. I walked point and slack, stood out on an LZ directing choppers, ran recon missions and retrieved bodies, but tunnel rat is not on my resume. Had I stayed longer, I'm sure I would have been involved in a situation where it had to be done. Throwing grenades into the bunker was the way we did it. Years later, we learned how extensive and impressive their tunnel system was, but I had just a passing knowledge of it at the time.

During one operation, our company spent a few days on top of a hill getting resupplied. Normally, we kept moving and didn't stay in one spot too long for fear the enemy would zero in on us. Of course, we conducted the usual patrols around the hill. After a few days, we left the area convinced that the enemy was not nearby.

A few weeks later a Ranger platoon (Rangers were highly trained soldiers, Special Forces like the Green Beret) were checking out that hill and they discovered that a hospital was set up in tunnels right under the top of the hill. Our company of 120 soldiers had spent about three days right on top of them and never knew that they were running a hospital with surgery, all right there under our noses.

The temperature was about 100 degrees and the water in our canteens was warm, but we drank it anyway. I thought a lot about getting a cold drink of water while playing in the back yard as a kid. We were supplied water with a blivet, a large rubber container. We used it to fill our canteens and to wash off. The NVA used it to make sandals. The enemy used a lot of our discards as weapons. They cut up metal and used them for booby traps. If we lost a grenade, they would use it against us. We secured our grenades so they didn't fall off while we were moving through the jungle.

In contrast to the 100 degree heat during the day, the temperatures at night in the mountains could drop as much as thirty to forty degrees. It was so cold that my poncho liner, a light blanket in a camouflaged color, was a savior to me. This had to be one of the Army's best inventions as it was light weight and took up little space.

Our rucksack was the most important item we carried, except for our rifle. It included four canteens of water and I added four more, so I carried eight pounds of just water. Plus, we carried four days of C-rations, for two meals a day. Ammo consisted of twenty-one magazines, each containing twenty rounds and a minimum of two grenades plus yellow, purple and red smoke grenades. Yellow and purple showed the choppers where to land, and the blowing smoke showed the direction of the wind while landing. Red was for an emergency, for example, if we had contact with the enemy.

As I settled into my role, I started carrying more grenades that I called "instant artillery" and eventually carried over a dozen. The total weight of my rucksack was 80 to 100 pounds plus a weapon of choice, typically an M-16. When first there, we carried mementos of home, but after a couple of days of hauling them up and down hills, we just carried the basics. I only weighed 150 pounds and, with the heat, food, canteens and ammunition, I was only going to carry what I needed.

For awhile, I carried a white phosphorous grenade but it was about the size of a junior high football and weighed much more than a regular grenade, which was about twenty-one ounces.

I thought I had a decent arm from playing outfield in softball, but this grenade could explode as far as sixty feet and I wasn't sure I could throw it far enough to escape the blast. I eventually sent it back to the rear.

In every squad of ten to twelve guys, each soldier had certain jobs. The RTO carried the radio for the squad leader. The military name of the radio was PRC-25 but we all called it a prick 25 and it weighed about twenty pounds, plus an extra battery. It was a tough job, but, come to think of it, they were all tough jobs.

The M-60 machine gun provided us with some great fire power, but it weighed about twenty pounds. The machine gunner had a crew that carried extra ammo and, when the fighting broke out, they were responsible for making sure his gun was fed with ammo without stopping. Usually, we all carried an extra can of M-60 ammo to have as much firepower as we could get.

Another job was manning the M-79 grenade launcher, a one shot at a time weapon that looked like a short barreled shotgun. We called it "thumper" because that's the sound it made when we shot it. Holly carried that and was very accurate with it. We used a regular explosive shell called HE, high explosive, or a flecchetee round that had darts in it to rip through the jungle and inflict damage on anything in its way.

Some U.S. units fought from a base camp and conducted search and destroy missions, then returned to the base camp for a beer and a meal. My assignment kept me in the field nearly all of the time. Weeks later, I visited the command center for our AO (Area of Operation) called a TOC, Tactical Operations Center. Ours was back at Camp Evans and underground, a safety measure to protect it from enemy mortars. While there, we saw how the war was just like a chess game. Troops were identified with one set of pins and the enemy another. We were inserted in one area to push the enemy into an ambush set up by another company. Going from point A to point B took good map reading, a skill I learned well at Ft. Benning. Of course, the real thing is a little different. There were numerous mountains in Nam and they all looked the same.

The Platoon Leader Lt. Ed Deuschle (pronounced dice-lee), and the Platoon Sergeant John Fraser and I got our maps out and compared information while nailing down our exact position. This was pre-GPS so we had to do all this manually. We wanted to make sure we were on the same page when it came to our location in the event of an attack. If we had to call in artillery we wanted to kill the enemy and not ourselves. Many deaths in the field were from friendly fire, and we didn't want to be a statistic.

There were times when the mountains confused us, causing artillery to fire at the wrong mountain. The first round fired would be white phosphorous or "Wilson Picket" as we called it, to pinpoint the target. It would explode about fifty yards over the target. That was the safety factor involved. If you saw the WP explode on the wrong target, you called off the mission. In some instances, they were prepared to fire directly at us before we called off the artillery.

The days were long, hot and sweaty. Moving through a thick jungle with a rucksack was slow and frustrating. The packs were always catching on vines, trees or other large plants. It was hilly terrain, which made it exhausting. When we stopped to take a break, even the warm water in a plastic canteen was satisfying. Some days we traveled just a short distance, perhaps 100 to 200 yards, and it took its toll on the body and mind.

When we were on top of a hill and took a break for chow, we established a day time perimeter of a big circle so we could see everyone. At night time, we set up a perimeter with a large circle of 9-10 positions of three men in each circle close enough so the enemy couldn't sneak between us. We knew that sappers were capable of quietly penetrating into our camp so we were especially careful at night. Guard duty started at 9:30 p.m. and went to around 6 a.m. There were usually three men to a position, alternating sleep times at night, pulling guard duty for an hour-and-a-half, twice a night. A third of the platoon was awake at one time. When we got attacked it was usually around 4:00 a.m. when it's hard staying awake. *Since my days in Nam, 4:00 a.m. always seems to be on the clock when I turn over in bed.*

Some duties had to be done before night fall. Number one was digging a foxhole large enough for three guys. When we first got into the field, we dug the hole to fit all of us. But, if we didn't have any contact with the enemy for awhile, we got lax in our digging.

One night, just after dark, we set up our fox holes, but we did not dig very deep. Then we heard a "thump," that sound you hear at fireworks displays, and we had a few seconds to find a safe place. We jumped into the hole that was supposed to hold all three of us, and pressed our flesh as close to the ground as we could. The first mortar round hit about fifty yards away, the next was about thirty yards away and the next was twenty. They were "walking in mortars" on us. After a minute, there was a pause.

When they paused, we started digging using an entrenching tool, which is a five inch shovel. In the next two minutes we dug a hole to fit three men comfortably. At the rate we were working, the three of us could have dug a basement in twenty minutes. We were scared shitless, but learned our lesson, until the next time. During the chaos of digging, we put on our helmets as quickly as we could. Edd Forrester and I looked at each other and we both laughed. I was laughing as he had put his helmet on backwards and he looked like Arty Johnson, the soldier on "Laugh In." He was laughing as I had put mine on backwards too. That is how Vietnam was; we had our good and bad times.

One guy hit something solid while digging a foxhole and realized he uncovered a shallow grave. He called me over and we saw that he hit a hand of a buried enemy soldier. I was told by the old heads that if we found any graves, we should keep it quiet, as our commanders in the rear would have us dig for other graves in the area so they could report a body count. Our guy moved his position over a few feet and he had a tough time sleeping near a dead body, but it beat the alternative.

A major function at night was setting up claymore mines to prevent the enemy from crawling up on us. Although claymores were also used by support units during the day and night, in the field, we used them when we established our perimeter each evening.

A claymore is about two pounds of C4, which is a little more powerful than dynamite. There are 600 BBs inside with a range of 50-100 meters. Claymores are about ten inches long by five inches high and an inch and a half thick. They are curved a little to spread out the blast. A wire with a blasting cap at the end is attached to the claymore mine and to a hand-held device we called the clicker.

We put claymores about ten feet in front of our position. If the enemy attacked, we squeezed the clicker and exploded it to neutralize the attacker. Ten feet is pretty close for two pounds of C4 but, if we put it too far out, the enemy could sneak up and turn it around. Then, if we hit the trigger, all the BBs would come back at us. Some guys put fluorescent tape on the back of the claymore at night so they could see if anyone messed with it. This was just another trick of the trade and a very important safety measure.

When the enemy lobbed in mortars and fired at us at night, not only were they trying to kill us, but they were also trying to provoke us to shoot back and use up our ammunition. Shooting at night exposed our position since our rifles gave off a big flash when shot. This enabled them to pinpoint our position and either lob in more mortars, or to send in sappers during the night or early morning. When we returned fire, we had to know when to stop shooting. Sometimes we would have to grab guys and make them quit shooting before they used up all their ammo.

We spent a lot of time just sitting around unable to move because prearranged air strikes or other troops were in the area. Bullets travel a long way so we didn't want to be down range. We played cards, and talked about sports.

We talked and thought about "Home." Often, soldiers had a calendar drawn on their helmets counting down the number of days remaining in-country. When they got to less than 100 days, they were a two digit midget. I figured out that I was going to be in Vietnam 525,600 minutes. I had the seconds figured out but I kept forgetting them. (31,536,000 seconds). My pay for all this was about 34 cents an hour. That's 24 hours a day, 30 days a month, do the math. (About $248 a month.)

Don resting in thick jungle

Don-Combat Ready

Recon-LRRP

About a month into the job as a squad leader, the CO (Commanding Officer) thought my going on reconnaissance would give me a broader understanding of the war. He wanted me to lead recon missions. I didn't know if this was a reward for my good work or I had said something to piss him off.

Recon consisted of six men traveling light for six days, and our firepower was limited to only M-16s and grenades. This small crew compared to a platoon of thirty to forty men and a company of three platoons with about 120 men. We used two radios--one to listen to battalion and the other to company radio conversations. Our job was to observe but not engage the enemy, and then report on their location and movements.

Technically, we were called Long Range Reconnaissance Patrols, (LRRPs), and pronounced Lurps. Ironically, one of the advantages to Recon was that we didn't eat C-rations, but Lurps instead. Lurps were meals in a pouch heated up with a cup of hot water. They were lighter and tastier than C-rations and there were no ham and lima beans. We ate lots of spaghetti. We considered Lurps the king of chow.

Quickly, five other guys volunteered for the mission, and I felt good that they placed their confidence in me. I was briefed by the battalion. I was provided a four-inch mirror that was to be used if the radios broke down and I was to shine it in the eyes of pilots flying over who, hopefully, would be coming to look for us.

Those on reconnaissance (recon) got dropped off on one hill and were picked up a week later on another hill. The six of us loaded onto a Huey chopper called a Slick, with three guys on each side. Two Cobra gun ships escorted us. Typically, the chopper would land or get close to the ground, and then we'd jump off. Sometimes we had just a few inches to jump and other times, when bullets were flying we might have a couple feet to jump to the ground. Jumping with a hundred pounds on our back was a hell of a jolt to the system. Then we ran to the tree line, and praying, not into an ambush.

When we went into an LZ, the direction of the chopper is 12 o'clock. We ran into the jungle at three and nine o'clock and met up at the predetermined 12 o'clock. The gun ships flying on either side of the chopper provided support as we ran to the tree line. They shot their miniguns a few feet in front of us trying to trip any booby traps or mines before we did. Of course, we worried that the gun ships would explode a mine just as we were running into it.

The first obstacles on the LZ were small tree stumps about two feet high and, while running for our life, our shins hit the hard tree stumps. Tree stumps on my bony shins really hurt. I thought that some day I was going to complain about them, but that was for another day. At that time, I just wanted to make it to the tree line.

Then, we had to avoid hostile fire while running to the tree line. While we ran, the hovering gun ships fired to protect us. The door gunner on the Huey shot at the tree line with rounds flying right over our heads or just to the side of us--literally inches away. The first thing the battalion would ask on the radio is whether it is a hot or cold LZ. Hot meaning the enemy is shooting at us or cold if they are not. With all that firepower, we couldn't tell who was firing, but we made it safely to the tree line.

We immediately moved away from the LZ. At night, we established our position. I took out my map and compass, looked at the terrain and tried to determine from what direction we could get attacked. We reviewed our maps in order to complete our duties of checking out a certain location for enemy activity. My training in map reading came in handy.

I figured out the coordinates of the likely avenue of attack and assigned them a number. I then contacted artillery support and we went over the coordinates and numbers so we were on the same page. For example, straight ahead of me would be target one. And instead of saying coordinates 482610, I'd say number one. Then I'd assign numbers around the circle. If we were attacked, it's a lot easier yelling out number four or five instead of coordinates. When bullets fly we had to be efficient, and the goal was to make it quick and simple.

While on recon, we avoided heavily trafficked trails, traveling slowly and very quietly. We kept talking to a minimum and communicated by hand signals and nods. The nonverbal communication was great among us and not much needed to be said for us to be on the same page. Occasionally, we heard the enemy close by, within twenty feet, and then it got real scary.

"Ain't it just like the night to play tricks when you're trying to be so quiet," Bob Dylan wrote. Sometimes we heard walking around us but we couldn't see anything. Everyone was poised for action. We frequently were breathing through our mouths rather than our noses to keep the noise down. We hoped they couldn't hear our hearts pounding. It was just so intense.

The jungle was thick and if the moon wasn't very bright it quickly got dark. When it gets dark in triple canopy jungle, it gets real dark. Triple canopy jungle has thick shrubs and bushes at body height, then another bunch of higher bushes covered by full trees higher up. This made it nearly impossible to see when the moon wasn't full. Sometimes we could barely see in front of us, unable to see our outstretched hands.

While preparing for the night, we ate later in the evening and then moved to another location for sleep just in case the enemy smelled or saw us. We usually tried to sleep under a tree off the trail where nobody walked. We rotated sleeping in one small circle with two guys up at a time.

We had to be super quiet. The TOC, which is battalion, would call every forty-five minutes for a sitrep, or situation report, to check on us. All questions were answered with a yes or no. We responded by clicking the receiver or 'breaking squelch' on the radio twice for yes (ok) and three times for no (trouble). We put the phone in our gut and curled over to minimize the noise that clicking a phone made.

When on recon, we sometimes traveled by base camps that were formerly occupied by GIs who had left a lot of garbage and, where there is garbage, there are rats. One night we set up in an area and hunkered down for the night after disposing of our leftover food.

When dark came we heard rustling in front of us and realized the noise was from rats. They were chomping on food and we heard their teeth gnawing on the empty cans. The rats were just a few feet in front of us and later they started chewing on our rucksacks. With just six of us, we were trying to maintain silence and not give away our position. We couldn't shoot them, but we kept butting the rats with our rifles. It was a horrible night and nobody got any sleep.

Not all nights were dark, and the nights when the moon was shining, we had a pretty clear vision of our surroundings. As noted, we were there to observe but not engage the enemy, and what we observed at night surprised me. Within a few minutes of the sunset, we sat back and saw the huge mountain across from us had hundreds of camp fires with an unknown number of enemy soldiers. I was curious how many were on our side of the valley. With just six of us, we were feeling very lonely.

Running out of water was a no-no, but when it's 100 degrees, it happens. One time, we cut soft trees with our machetes that we thought were banana trees and sucked the moisture from them. We saw streams that looked like fresh water but were advised not to drink it because the CIA had poisoned the stream. It appeared to be true as we saw dead fish floating. But when it got so hot with no water, we took a chance and drank it. In World War II, the machine guns were water cooled and when the weather got hot, the soldiers drank the dirty water. The Army fixed that by designing the weapons to be air cooled so we no longer had that option.

One day, while sitting in the jungle listening to the two radios with one radio in one ear listening to activity in the company and the other ear for battalion activity. A jet was heading back to the base and the pilot called in and he wanted to get rid of a bomb he had left. He didn't want to land with a couple hundred pound bomb strapped to his underbelly, so he asked battalion where he could drop it. They gave out the coordinates where to drop it and I looked at the map and noticed that it was pretty close to our position. So I hurriedly called up TOC and said "Hey, remember, we are out here."

I vividly recall how casual the conversation was on the radio when he told the pilot, "Oh yeah, better not drop it out there, I got a LRRP team in the area." Fortunately, they picked another target.

Another time, we listened all night when our platoon that we just left for recon had an artillery strike hit them with friendly fire. It was a "danger close mission," that is, when the Army fires artillery real close to the troops. Five guys were wounded and one was killed. The chaos of the night was played over the radio.

They were calling in "Dustoff 92," a medevac to come and extract everyone. A night time extraction is difficult and I listened as they were going back and forth on the radio. The pilot was trying to get in and at least get a seriously wounded GI out and it just wasn't going well. In the background, they were telling the guy to hang on. Finally about four a.m., a dejected voice came on the radio and told the pilot to come back in the morning and pick up the body. We just sat there helpless as this was going on.

Each morning, the TOC would ask us about the weather and how high in the mountains the clouds were located. This provided valuable information on when and if they could send choppers out to various sites. Of course, the day we were scheduled to be picked up, we told them it was a clear day. We may have stretched the truth somewhat just to get the hell out of there. The pilots laughed when they arrived and saw the fog surrounding us, waiting for our ride home. Hey, six days out in the jungle was no fun, and very scary.

Recon was a great experience for me as it accelerated my awareness of the terrain and the enemy movements. I only participated in a couple of these missions.

Mike Campbell, a friend, and Jack Lemmon, who I worked with at the Post Office for years after Vietnam, did recon all the time. Don't ever sneak up on them as their response might be slower today but still more reactionary than one would expect from a civilian.

Don with Rosary, P-38, back up watch around neck.

Back from Recon, on bunker, outside the wire.

Sergeant John Fraser

Back in the Field

After being on recon for awhile it took time to adjust back to the platoon. With just six of us on recon, we had to be real quiet. But, with thirty or so guys it wasn't very quiet, as hard as we tried.

On top of our eighty-pound rucksack we were ordered to carry a LAW, Light Anti Tank Weapon, usually strapped across the top of our gear. It seemed they always got caught on the jungle vines. We used them against enemy bunkers as we were in the mountains where no tanks or anything mechanized operated. These LAW's used one shot artillery shell and operated like a WWII Bazooka with surprising accuracy. We had to dispose of the LAWs after firing or the enemy would use them for booby traps.

Our platoon also carried a "starlight scope" which allowed us to see the enemy at night. This was newly developed and in the early stages of usage. It was particularly helpful on a clear night as it used the moon and stars for light. On cloudy nights it was not very effective, and it was cumbersome to carry. After a few nights of not being able to use it coupled with a cloudy forecast, some soldiers got frustrated and smacked it against the tree and sent it in for repairs so they didn't have to carry it. Some guys said it made a whining sound, but what I heard was broken glass after it hit the tree.

I was the first squad leader at this time and tried to keep everyone moving and quiet. I just got back from recon and I wasn't used to the elevated noise. Guys were swearing about walking through the jungle. It was slow and tedious and we used our machetes to cut through the thick jungle. The guys got frustrated in the heat and with the vines catching on our rucksacks and LAWs.

I said, "Keep it down, Charlie will hear you." Charlie was the name we gave to enemy soldiers. This one guy was angry at the conditions yells out, "Fuck Charlie, fuck this place, and fuck everything." I started laughing and said, "So much for sneaking up on anybody." Everybody laughed. The guy came over later and apologized about his outburst and we had another good laugh.

The name for the VC, or Viet Cong, was termed by the military as Victor Charlie. Other terms used might be Charlie Foxtrot, which was another way to say "Cluster Fuck."

Search and destroy missions were controversial. That is, U.S. troops patrolled designated areas expecting to encounter the enemy and, with artillery and chopper support, inflict more casualties than suffered. These search and destroy missions put our troops in danger of an ambush that could result in a number of fatalities. However, without them, the enemy would have been able to get much closer to our bases and cause even greater damage to the troops, ammo and helicopters. Later, these search and destroy missions became search and avoid as nobody wanted to be killed.

Our platoon leader was Lieutenant Ed "Rebel" Deuschle. Ed had attended "Ole Miss" on a baseball scholarship. They played Auburn for the SEC championship in 1967 and lost the final game. He was a good leader and taught me many valuable lessons during those unbelievable and taxing times. Ed was always well prepared for our next encounter and was our calm voice in the storm. And trust me, there were some storms.

John Fraser was the platoon sergeant from Maine. He really worked with me on all phases of the job. This combat stuff seemed like a natural for him, but not to me. We played a lot of cards, mostly rummy, and I owed him a lot of beers. He was like the other guys; we were all in this together. We talked about a lot of things.

My RTO at this time was Edd Forrester, a great guy who really helped me. He was terrific at his job and was a stable influence during chaos. His advice was invaluable to me and he was able to put it all in proper perspective.

Don Goss was my point man. When I came back from recon, Don asked me to walk slack for him. Don explained how he wanted me to react if we made contact with the enemy. I was to fire across his back and to the left because he would be firing low and to the right, the natural kick of the rifle. He was a great point man and I felt honored that he trusted me backing him up.

We rotated the point job as sometimes people had a feeling about that day and we trusted their judgment. My squad walked point for the company a lot. One day, Jim Garner from New Jersey was the point man and the jungle was particularly thick. He stopped, and we could feel it in the air that something was up. He motioned to me.

I stopped and took a step back to say something to Edd, the RTO, when a grenade went off about five feet from me. The concussion knocked me down. Everybody went down fast with smoke and dirt and leaves flying through the air. The NVA had just ambushed us, and automatic fire was all around. I was so scared that I felt for my legs but I couldn't feel anything. I thought they were gone but, in reality, I couldn't have felt my face as I was too numb from shock.

Paralysis is a killer in combat, but so is making stupid moves. I was lying there and heard the NVA empty their AK-47s at us. Bullets coming at us seemed to scream as they pierced the air. I could hear the metal on metal as the rounds were sliding into the enemy chamber. I heard another reload a magazine and start firing. It seemed like forever, but it was just a few seconds. It is like in a baseball game when the pitcher throws the ball and you get a second to think about swinging at it. If you are a second late, it is already in the catcher's mitt. I was facing Nolan Ryan. Welcome to the major leagues.

We returned fire. In war movies you see guys taking aim at a target. But in the beginning of a real ambush, we put our rifles over our heads and just tried to get some rounds in the enemy's direction so they would put their heads down and quit shooting. I had a lot of grenades so I threw some in the direction of the NVA. We had to be careful throwing grenades in a thick jungle because if it hit a tree it could bounce back and explode near us.

Ed or John started calling in gun ships. As I waited, I figured that the enemy threw a grenade at me and the tree took the brunt of the explosion. If I hadn't taken a step back to talk with Edd, I would have taken more of the blast. It made me think about divine intervention.

Platoon Sergeant Fraser came up as we started to pop smoke grenades. We directed the gun ships to hit the enemy just a few yards in front of us, just to the north of the smoke. Those gun ships did a great job in that thick jungle. During that ambush, nobody was hurt and we considered ourselves all pretty lucky. We looked for dead enemy but didn't find any. That battle was a draw.

Later, we sat around and talked about the day. It was a surreal conversation. I remember somebody saying "War is hell" and then Don Goss finishing it with what we always said when we heard that, "And combat is a motherfucker." We always chuckled when we heard that, just wanting to diffuse our situation.

Booby traps were all over the place. Once, we were moving around in an area and then suddenly, on the radio, we were told not to move. A point man from another platoon had just found a booby trap with about six 81mm shells strung together. They were lined down a path about ten meters apart. If the point man had tripped the wire, the shells would have done major damage. Sometimes when I walked point, I would be so cautious that when I approached a spider web I rubbed it between my finger and thumb to make sure it wasn't a wire.

We were resupplied with C-rations about every three to four days. Food was not that good. C-rations were tolerable and, after awhile, I came to enjoy the pork and beans as well as the spaghetti. C-rations got special nicknames. Some meals like ham and lima beans were just flat out unappealing and we called them ham and motherfuckers. When the cases of C's came in, there was a lot of trading going on. Occasionally, they would drop us some beers, but they were usually warm.

C-ration meals came in cans with a main course like spaghetti in the size of a soup can, crackers were in a ¾ inch high can, and a small can contained cheese or peanut butter. There was a plastic spoon, a small pack of four cigarettes and a little pack of toilet paper. And the most important tool of every infantryman in the field was a P-38, or a can opener. We wore it around our necks along with a rosary that many of us kept.

The P-38 was small and the larger beer can opener was the P-52, after the B-52 bombers that flew over us and dropped bombs on the enemy.

Usually we ate just two meals a day, so we supplemented them with snacks--sometimes candy bars. There was a chocolate bar we called the John Wayne bar. It was chocolate designed not to melt in hot weather and it had a really bad taste. You had to be a real trooper and hungry to eat it.

But we could craft a good snack out of all the stuff we got. We had packets of chocolate and we made hot chocolate by adding dried cream and sugar packets to improve the taste. We used fast burning C4 explosive to make the hot chocolate instantly. C4 was also very expensive, about $50 for a two pound bar. C4 was about the size of one of those huge Milky Way bars found at truck stops. We peeled just a little piece, about the size of a chewed piece of gum, and lit it. We'd stir in all the ingredients and, voila, we had the world's most expensive hot chocolate. It wasn't bad.

Speaking of food, which we did a lot, occasionally they shipped out a hot meal to us. I was told that it cost about $1.50 a meal for C-rations and 35 cents for a hot meal. The idea of a hot meal sounded great but, in reality, it was not what it was cracked up to be. First, the food arrived in a used artillery canister, a two foot long plastic tube lined with a plastic bag that once held an artillery shell. Sounds tasty already, don't it? The meals that I remember were mashed potatoes, gravy and a meat. When I say a meat, that is what it was. It had no other name except meat. It was a collection of various meats pressed together. Eat enough C's, and meat has a nice sound to it.

When we were in the field we used special codes to request a hot meal for the squad or platoon. For security purposes, we didn't say a number over the radio. We tried to be as tricky so the enemy wouldn't know the size of our force. When I ordered for my squad of sixteen, I requested enough for two baseball teams, or a football team and a basketball team.

If somebody in my squad needed something from the rear, I called it in using a line number issued to everyone before they went out to the field. Mine was 189, and Edd, my RTO, was 178. I would say 189 needs new shoes or grenades, and the next time the chopper came out they brought it. We didn't want the enemy to get our name as they could use it for propaganda, causing a lot of discomfort to our family.

Sometimes, the choppers couldn't land so they hovered over us and pushed out the supplies. A case of C's weighed about thirty pounds and if that dropped from the sky and hit someone, it could do some damage. Yes, some guys got hit and it hurt. We joked that guys were taken out by a case of pork and beans.

Other times, there wasn't room for the choppers to even toss out the food or a medevac chopper to land to take out the wounded, and we had to create a LZ. We all had C4 on us and used it to blow down enough trees for the chopper to land. We had a bunch of young soldiers with highly dangerous explosives but we took it seriously and carefully planned our approach. The C4 was pliable and would bend to fit the shape of the tree. It had a peel-off that had a sticky side that we put on a tree. We inserted a blasting cap into an end and hit the clicker from the claymore mines to blow it.

I wasn't sure how much C4 to use and my first attempt didn't do much damage to a tree. A couple of the old heads helped me and we packed a lot more firepower to the next one and blew it to smithereens, wherever that is. Whenever we were ready to blow the C4, we yelled, "fire in the hole" at least three times to warn the other guys and they cleared out of the area. This process could take hours to clear the LZ before the choppers could get in.

After securing the LZ, the choppers arrived with the cargo and we divvied up the food and other stuff and then got moving. Food from home was a gift. My mother sent stuff to me and it was great. Joe Vetrano, a friend of mine who I visited at Ohio University before I came over, sent me a care package. It had all kinds of goodies in it. The package looked as though the post office had played a game of soccer with it. The Oreo cookies were so crunched up that we ate them with a spoon. All the guys in the unit sat around and polished off the goodies. To this day, I'm so appreciative of what Joe sent me.

There was a toilet behind every tree, and that's where we went along with an entrenching tool and toilet paper. We had to make sure we took our rifle with us as we didn't want to get caught with our pants down without our weapon. Of course, a good reason to move to another area was that if we stayed too long, we were surrounded by a huge toilet.

The thick jungle was always moist and when the monsoons hit, it was worse. We pretty much had to put up with the rain, just sitting in the jungle with it showering down for days. We were soaked to the bone all the time. I remember taking my socks off and rubbing my skin and it just flaked off.

The main challenge was to keep our M-16s well oiled and in good working condition, especially with all the dampness. We poured LSA lubricant on the rifle, ensuring that it didn't jam. A lot of problems were reported, but mine worked well.

Occasionally, the lieutenant let us put up our waterproof ponchos like a tent. The poncho was shiny like rain gear, so a little haze from the sun or moon would give off a glare that the enemy could target in on. So in certain conditions, we had to take the makeshift tent down and just sit there in the downpour.

One time, Sergeant Fraser and I were sitting in the rain talking about everything under the sun, or clouds in this case. It was pouring all around and we were about to go to sleep on the wet ground. We just finished eating some C-rations and were talking about who was living worse than us now.

We agreed some third world countries had nothing at all, but just about everybody in the good old USA was doing better than us. We were feeling down about our situation. Then the enemy started lobbing mortar shells at us so we hit the ground and climbed in our wet fox holes. A few rounds had gone off and then the shelling stopped as quickly as it started. I looked at John and said, "We never knew how good we had it." We laughed.

When it was so wet, there were other things to worry about. One morning I got up and soon felt a little sluggish. The uniforms had laces in the bottom of pants to keep unwanted creatures out. I looked down and noticed a rip in my pants.

As I looked closer, there was a leech sucking on my leg. So, of course, the first thing a sergeant in the 101st Airborne wants to do is yell, "Mom!" The leeches got my full attention, so I pulled my pant leg up and there were more of those suckers. I jumped up and dropped my pants and about a dozen were all over my leg. If we just flicked them off, the head stays in the body and the leg gets infected. We had to burn them off or squirt bug juice on them.

Once everyone saw what was going on they gathered around and started burning them off with their cigarettes. It took a few minutes to get all of them off. Unfortunately this wasn't the last time I had to deal with leeches in Vietnam, but never as many as that day. I still cringe just thinking about it.

Taking showers was a rare event. A modified clean up was to use a stream to wash off our bodies. Even then it was dangerous as we could be ambushed. We took turns washing off while other guys stood guard. We used a minimum amount of soap because it gives off a strong smell that could identify our location.

Mosquitoes were especially problematic during the dry season. To repel them, we used bug juice that we carried in the strap of our helmet. It was about the size of hotel shampoo. We sprayed this "Off" all over our exposed flesh and our face, and it was like makeup. Since we didn't wash every day, it caked up and I felt like Phyllis Diller.

Cigarettes were especially helpful when trying to eat. I wasn't a smoker but I used the four cigarettes to ward off the mosquitoes. We couldn't take a bite of food without gulping at least one bug. They didn't like the smoke and fire, so we put a lighted cigarette in one side of our mouth and put food in the other to get a bite of food without a mouthful of mosquitoes.

While traveling through an area where a skirmish had taken place, we looked at equipment left behind. We didn't pick up anything for fear of a booby trap. The enemy would attach a grenade to a flag or souvenir. A GI helmet with a crucifix on the front had a bullet hole right below Jesus and his outstretched arms. Everyday we prayed for the best but when I saw that, I just thought, "Oh, man, this is not good."

Firebases

Periodically, about once a month, each company rotated from the field to firebases to protect them and to give us a little break from the action. We were assigned to FSB Rakkason, a more secure area than the bush.

We were sent back to a firebase to let us reorganize, rest up a little and get clean uniforms. In the field, we pretty much wore the same clothes every day. On a firebase, there were clean clothes, but they were used, and were stacked in piles. We rummaged through the piles to find our size.

Being on a firebase was good duty. We could take a shower. We heated up the water and poured it into five gallon pails with holes in the bottom that drizzled water on us. This "Australian" shower required us to lather up real quick and rinse off as quickly. It was effective and it felt great.

We went to the bathroom right out in front of everybody into 55 gallon barrels cut in half. After we filled it up we poured diesel fuel into it, started it on fire and stirred. The job was called Honey-dipper. Sounds like a real sweet job. That's how the Army did things, make it sound like something you'll volunteer for and bam, the next thing you know, you got a real shitty job.

A firebase was out in the jungle on an LZ to provide artillery support for the soldiers in the field. Firebases were strategically placed all over the area. Smaller firebases had 105 Howitzer guns and larger ones had 155 Howitzers. The bigger the gun, the further they could support the troops. Once the distances that artillery could cover were established, ground troops on patrol would not go beyond these limits or they would lose fire support. The enemy knew this when they planned their attacks and wanted to be beyond our firepower support, but that didn't happen very often.

The down side of firebases was that the enemy liked to attack them with sappers trying to penetrate the wire with the intent to blow up everything and to kill soldiers. Concertina wire contained sharp razor blades to deter the sappers.

When on duty, we were positioned outside the wire as the first line of defense. Actually, we had wire down the hill protecting us somewhat. At night, the last thing we wanted to hear was "gooks in the wire," as it meant we were being attacked.

If other firebases had been under attack in the area and intelligence informed our commanders that an attack was likely, they occasionally ordered a "mad minute." This is where everyone would fire into the jungle with all weapons at the same time for about a minute. Often, this occurred about three to four a.m., the likely time for an assault. If nothing else happened, it got everyone awake.

We were on FSB Rakkason in late April or early May when all the firebases were getting hit. Our duties included being on LP or OP. Listening Post (LP) was a night time activity where three guys with a radio were positioned outside the protection of the wire, perhaps 100-300 feet. They were concealed in brush hiding from the enemy and were to alert the firebase if the enemy was approaching. The Observation Post (OP) was a day-time activity with the same general duties. The first few days on Rakkason we went without LPs as our commanders were convinced that we were going to be attacked and didn't want anyone stranded outside the wire. This is when they called for a "mad minute."

To ensure there weren't gaps in the perimeter where the enemy could penetrate between us, we dug additional bunkers and manned them with just two guys instead of the usual three. One night, another guy and I had a M-79 grenade launcher and we fired it into the jungle at various times throughout the night. To make us feel safer, we played a game where we fired one into the air and then fired straight ahead to see how many we could fire before the first one hit the ground. This was also called "Recon by fire," that is, instead of walking through an area, we blew it up from a distance.

Some firebases were permanent, but many were abandoned during the monsoon season because we couldn't resupply them with choppers due to the heavy fog and rain.

When it rained, helicopters didn't fly as much, so we relied on artillery alone. We coordinated activities to ensure our support units knew our position as well as others fighting in the area. Usually, there were a number of companies and battalions nearby.

Large Chinook helicopters delivered artillery guns to the desired locations, often to a mountaintop. These helicopters pilots delivered all types of support material and the dangerous ones carried fuel for generators. The biggest fear of a helicopter pilot was taking a hit with fuel on board and being burned to death. *Charlie Notarianni was a door gunner on a Chinook chopper for eighteen months, and he later worked next to me at the post office in Ashtabula.*

These Chinook choppers also provided other resources. The Army tried to make life a little better on a firebase. They flew a rock band out to us loaded on what we called a "shithook" Chinook chopper. They had generators to power the electric guitars and played while we drank some beers. There were no women but occasionally they sent out some "Doughnut Dollies", some twenty something year old American girls who volunteered to come out and talk with the soldiers. It was nice of them to do that and it was a morale booster.

Although I wasn't around at Christmas time when Bob Hope and the USO brought over entertainment, I read that Raquel Welch, after returning from a trip to Vietnam, said that she didn't want to go back. She felt her performance was like waving red meat in front of a caged tiger. She was sympathetic to our plight and she said the Army should bring in whore houses and let the men have at it. But, that is life on a firebase.

FSB Rakkason

FSB Rakkason up close

FSB Maureen

Before we CA'd (Combat Assault) into Firebase Maureen there was a church service for the whole company that all three platoons attended. Having been raised a Catholic, I understood my religion. I was taught, more or less, that our way was the only way to God. That morning on FSB Rakkason a minister was saying mass. We called all chaplains "sky pilot" no matter what denomination they were.

David Heino, brother to a good friend of mine, Liz Lyons, was originally from Ashtabula. He was a chaplain in the Army stationed at Camp Evans, one of the largest base camps in the northern region. He was the son of a minister and brother to Ruth Heino, a classmate of my brother Mark in high school. A few years back, David was visiting Liz and her husband Dave. We discussed our time in Vietnam as we both served in the same area. I better understood the anguish that chaplains endured listening to the men talk about their fears and deeds while in the heat of battle. David was wounded and hospitalized for a long time from injuries received in Vietnam. He died from cancer a few years ago as did his sister Ruth. His family remains good friends of mine.

The minister said he didn't care what religion we were, he wanted us to take communion before this mission. I listened to what he said, and realized God opened up many avenues of access to Him and some religions simply had better marketing skills than others. In a few hours, I was praying to God for some help, whoever He was.

On the 5th of May 1970, our company was going to CA into FSB Maureen. It was early morning and we got all our gear ready. About twenty helicopters were coming to get us. Captain Don Workman, a West Point graduate known as Ranger, met with the three platoon leaders. I was 1st squad leader for 3rd platoon.

For communication, we had call names for each platoon and squad. Lima, Mike, and November were platoon names for first, second and third platoon respectively.

First squad leader was one, second squad two and third squad was three. At the time, I was in the 3rd platoon, 1st squad leader so my name was November 1.

My radio man for the squad was Romeo, so his name was November 1, Romco, or November 1, R. The platoon sergeant was November 5 and the platoon leader, a lieutenant, was November 6. Normally, we ran three platoons and two squads in each platoon due to the shortage of troops.

Captain Workman said the operation was a body counting mission. The area was bombed by the Air Force. The Navy used the New Jersey, a World War II battleship, and fired shells the size of a VW bug into the area. Artillery was prepping the LZ all night.

Firebase Maureen

A few days earlier, south of us, the 1st Cavalry had invaded Cambodia. We were going just east of Laos, where the Ho Chi Minh Trail was located. It was a network of roads built from North Vietnam to South Vietnam through the countries of Laos and Cambodia.

It provided logistical support to the VC and the NVA. It was a combination of truck routes and paths for foot and bicycle traffic. When all the various routes were totaled, the trail was actually 16,000-kilometers (9,940-miles) long.

When on Recon, I saw how freely the enemy moved and remembered all the campfires. The enemy read our newspapers and was aware the U.S. was facing protestors and the military had their hands tied by politicians. The NVA knew we had our limits on what we could do and where we could go, putting us at a disadvantage. If we went into Cambodia or Laos, we would be accused of escalating the war which is, of course, what happened.

We should have bombed the hell out of the trail and we should have done it at the beginning of the war. I knew that on college campuses around the country, students were protesting the bombing of Cambodia but, in my opinion, it was long overdue. When you get into a war, either fight like hell to win, or get out. The reality was that Nixon had been secretly bombing Cambodia for more than a year.

"Back in the world," as we used to say, the bombing of Cambodia caused several protests on campuses, notably Kent State where my brother Pat and my friends were attending at that time. On May 4, 1970, the protests escalated resulting in the infamous shooting of thirteen kids; four were killed and nine were injured.

As mentioned, we were told to go in and count bodies on FSB Maureen after the firepower from the Air Force and Navy plus our own artillery pounded on it. We expected this to be a rather routine mission. What happened to us that day was, sad to say, a real screw up of epic proportions.

First, we learned later that the heavy fire to the landing zone was to the secondary LZ. Second, we should have been suspicious as the Kit Carson scouts were not around as we were heading out to Maureen. Kit Carson scouts, also called Chu hois, which means surrender, were former NVA soldiers who changed allegiances and worked for us, pointing out problem areas. Any time they felt threatened or thought we were going into an enemy stronghold, they would bail out. They would have been killed if they were captured by the NVA, and it would have been a brutal death.

After boarding the twenty-one Huey choppers and approaching our landing site, the 3rd platoon, mine, was the first one to land on the LZ. There were three choppers on one pad and two choppers on the other pad with six men on each chopper. As the thirty of us were getting off the choppers, the enemy was literally sitting on the LZ looking at us. Since this was supposed to be a well planned mission, we were surprised when met by the large enemy force. They fully expected the choppers to just keep flying by once we recognized that it was occupied, but we swooped down and landed instead.

Edd Forrester, my RTO, took two steps off the chopper and shot two NVA who were no more than fifteen feet from us. I was on the radio informing our commanders that we had a hot LZ. Within seconds, we were all down and spread out on the ground and popping red smoke indicating a hot LZ. At the same time, Lt. "Rebel" Deuschle and Sergeant Fraser were also calling in to report the heavy resistance. Al Collins, the other squad leader on the other side of the mountain top had enemy all around his men.

On the radio, they wanted to know how many were there but we were so spread out on all sides of the mountain we couldn't tell. We were barely able to keep track of who was right in front of us. I wasn't catering the event so I didn't care about the numbers. I just wanted help. The other choppers wouldn't land because of the heavy combat. If they tried and got shot down, they could lose their men, and there was a good chance of crashing on top of us and causing even more damage. It was so bizarre to be trapped on that hill with nobody to help us and no way out. It was just our platoon and we were dodging bullets the entire time. It was a blur to me and I only remember some snippets of the situation. I guess the mind shuts down when you are in the "flight or fight" mode, and I definitely wasn't able to flight to anywhere.

Lieutenant Deuschle (right) was the only officer on the ground. He had taken quite a jolt jumping off the chopper and jammed his leg. He mobilized us to areas of the LZ to protect us and spent a lot of time on the radio coordinating the return fire. We were taking fire from three different positions  and the enemy had us pinned down. They were mortaring us and hitting us with gas. We hadn't used our gas mask since basic training and we were scrambling to put them on while we kept shooting. There were many wounded and killed.

I lost my grenadier Hollingsworth (Holly). He was hit either by a sniper or friendly fire while running from the chopper after we landed. The door gunners on our choppers were firing their machine guns and the chopper pilot's front window was hit with rifle fire. Perhaps, when he jerked the chopper, the door gunner shot across Holly's back. In the heavy fighting, it is unclear what really happens. When he went down, I thought he was a goner.

Holly & Don

The medic got to him in time and the medevac team came in a little later and took him out. Medics came in with a big red cross painted on their side which meant the enemy wasn't supposed to fire on them, but they didn't care, and shot at them all the time.

We were trapped for over an hour until we secured the area and brought in the rest of the company. I can't say enough good things about Lt. Deuschle, Sgt. Fraser and my RTO Edd Forrester. They handled this like pros. Edd Forrestor was awarded the Bronze Star for bravery in this mission. Finally, we got everyone together on top of FSB Maureen and we spent the first night as one big unit. We were licking our wounds and hoping the worst was over, but it wasn't.

The next morning, May 6th, three platoons patrolled the area and once again made contact with the enemy. Later, the 1st Platoon came back and covered the northern part of the mountain top, a considerable distance from the 2nd platoon. Captain Workman had us, the 3rd platoon, move off the hill about fifty yards on the steep side of the hill and he traveled with us. Lt. Deuschle was the leader of our platoon and the captain was in charge of the entire company. We set up our position and dug in for the night.

Lt. Fletcher's 2nd Platoon stayed on top of the hill. Some questioned this decision as they were making camp at the same place as the previous night. This was unusual and against all conventional wisdom. The enemy has gauged their position and could more easily plan an attack.

Also, with such a large area to protect, the 2nd Platoon coverage was very thin, leaving large gaps between the men on guard duty. The 2nd Platoon was undermanned with four on medical leave and one or two guys were on R&R. This left only twenty-one guys covering an area fifty yards long and thirty yards wide. They only had ten two-man foxholes. Some argued that the entire company should have remained together as the terrain was difficult but passable and vulnerable to attack.

On the morning of May 7th, the enemy hit the 2nd Platoon from the northwest and west sides with a lot of heavy gunfire right away. The NVA's way of operating was hit and run and they launched their sapper units into the camp. Sappers carried satchel charges of explosives about five square inches and a couple inches wide with fuses lit and timed to explode as they reached our guys. The enemy had a well planned attack when they struck that morning.

They knew where people were located as they immediately went for Lt. Fletcher and his radioman, Ken David. They killed Lt. Fletcher immediately. David escaped injury and played a pivotal role in the ensuing battle. Ironically, a few days earlier, Lt. Fletcher received a "Dear John" letter and was scheduled for an R&R, but he wanted to be with his troops.

Some of those who took the initial hit kept the enemy at bay. Steve "the Greek" Avgerinos was near Lt. Fletcher and got on the radio to Captain Workman, and called for air and artillery support. Ken David and Greg Phillips took a position on the west side firing machine guns and throwing grenades while sending up trip flares so the gun ships could fire at the enemy.

Ken Kays, a medic, was new to the unit and was pushed into action that morning. He helped a couple guys, but when he went to assist another, he was hit by a mortar.

He got up but tumbled, and then he realized that his left leg below the knee was gone. He wrapped it in a tourniquet, gave himself two shots of morphine and continued to help others. His bravery under attack and selfless actions would be rewarded with the Medal of Honor.

Greg Phillips and Ken David were so near the enemy that a satchel charge thrown by hand landed a couple feet from them and, when it blew, they both got hit with shrapnel. They also had an RPG pass between them and exploded behind them. Another satchel charge landed right in front of them but it failed to go off. At about the same time, a NVA soldier was pointing an AK-47 rifle at Phillips and he instinctively fired his grenade launcher. It takes about fifteen feet and enough revolutions for a grenade to activate and explode. The guy was so close that Greg basically shot him with just the shell and hit him square in the face, killing him instantly.

We heard the attack on 2nd platoon about 4:00 a.m. Our platoon was about fifty yards south but on the side of a steep hill. Captain Workman ordered us to blow our claymore mines and head up the hill to support the 2nd platoon. I crawled to my squad and repeated the orders. The first group heard me say "blow the claymore" and, a second later, they blew it and knocked me back a couple feet. Two pounds of C4 blown up only about ten feet away has a concussion to it. I got a chuckle out of this, so when I crawled up to the next position, I rephrased my order. I said "When I leave, blow the claymore and we'll go up the hill." That let me get a few feet away before they blew it.

Our platoon was crawling up the side of the barren hill that was wide open with no jungle for cover. Scrambling up the steep hill was difficult and we soon got fired on. The assault prevented us from making good time up the side of the mountain to help the 2nd Platoon.

By this time, some support was coming in, mainly choppers that were dropping flares to light the night, like the illumination from a 4th of July fireworks show. The lighting was not very bright but it helped identify objects, mainly us on the side of the hill.

We could hear the machine gun fire, sapper charges going off and the choppers firing into the enemy locations. We wanted to get up there as quickly as possible but we faced our own challenges.

The enemy was hiding in the jungle and we were exposed on the side of a hill. They could see us much better than we could see them. They started to mortar and shoot at us and the mortars were blowing up above and below us. If a mortar blows up above me the shrapnel blows over me. If it blows below me the shrapnel goes into the side of the hill. If it hits me, I'm done.

We finally got up the hill and bodies were everywhere, ours and theirs. Lt. Deuschle was one of the first on the scene and he tossed a grenade and killed two sappers. The sappers were in a battle with another sergeant, but Deuschle ended it before they could blow their satchel charges. Sergeant Fraser had me and my squad take over a machine gun position. My squad was firing into the jungle with everything we had; machine guns, M-16s, and grenade launchers. The choppers above were firing at the enemy, and it was hectic.

I was in a foxhole and started shooting nonstop, and the sound was hard on my ears. After a few minutes, my eardrums started hurting. I had to keep shooting and my ears felt like they were gushing with blood. I pushed my right shoulder into my right ear, thinking this would keep me from bleeding so much. I figured if I could just stop half the bleeding, I would last a little longer. In fact, I wasn't bleeding at all; I had just blown my eardrums out.

We were running out of ammo, so I crawled around looking for more on the bodies of the guys who were killed just minutes earlier. I crawled up and stared at them for what seemed a long time. I couldn't believe they were dead. I had just had a beer with some of them back at the base camp. I can still see their faces. Some had the ammo strapped on them like Poncho Villa, so I stripped the bandoliers from them and threw it to the guys who were manning their positions.

Sergeant Fraser told me to take my squad on a patrol around the base of the hill at daybreak. As he was talking to me, a bullet bounced off his helmet.

Instead of dropping to the ground, we both stayed on our knees talking, just moving another foot or so to take the angle away from the enemy. Later, I talked with John about this and he didn't recall the incident, but he didn't deny it either.

Finally, the enemy retreated back into the jungle and, after the fighting stopped, we assessed the damage. Ken Kays, the medic, was found on the side of the hill covering two guys who were wounded. We realized that he continued to help others after losing a leg.

A soldier was screaming about how his legs hurt. Two satchel charges were thrown into his foxhole during the battle and he was unable to get out before they blew, yet he continued to fire his machine gun. When he was pulled from the foxhole, his legs were gone. When the choppers arrived, we loaded him on one, but not with his legs. I remember watching his chest and squinting my eyes to see if he was still breathing as the chopper flew out. I read later that it was Peter Cook. Ed Deuschle told me this was one of the worst images of the war for him. He jumped in the foxhole with Peter and all Pete could do was wiggle his finger to communicate. He was close to death before he was put on the chopper, and when he discovered his legs were missing, he went into shock and died.

In a short time, it was daybreak, and I had orders to take my squad out on a patrol. Heading down the hill, I saw one NVA sapper laying there and his head looked as though someone had taken a paring knife to his face and carved it out. I thought for many years that he had been hit from behind by an M-16, because a bullet from it will blow a hole the size of a basketball in anything it hits. Greg Philips told me later that he shot the guy with a grenade launcher that didn't explode.

The patrol continued and the enemy bodies were all over the base of the hill. Guys were shooting the bodies, they said, to make sure they were dead but they were really letting out some frustration. I was not about to argue. We found about twenty unexploded satchel charges, representing about one-third of the total that went off. We gathered the charges and detonated them.

At this point, everyone was a little shocked. A couple of older guys, about 24, approached the company commander. I was about thirty feet away and I didn't hear everything, but I heard enough. They suggested that we call in choppers and get out of there. Captain "Ranger" Workman slapped one of them and told them to get back to their positions. He said, "I could shoot you right here if I wanted to." He wanted to quell any type of morale problem. Looking back, the older guys were right, but we all followed our leader.

After the battle, we realigned our company. We lost our 2nd Platoon Leader, Lt. Fletcher and a new sergeant Redmond. Seven GIs were killed that night and many wounded leaving only about six soldiers in 2nd platoon, so they joined the 1st platoon. So now we had only two platoons, and were stretched even thinner.

At that time, we did not know the enemy's strength. Later, we discovered that going into FSB Maureen, we were outnumbered by 1,200 to 120. We landed in an area of the 803rd NVA, and an elite sapper group had a major base just south of Maureen.

Due to the loss of men, they canceled all leave, including any scheduled R&Rs. Nobody was allowed to go to the rear as we were short on men and we needed as many as possible. After Maureen, each day was one of walk a little and watch for ambushes. One day my squad was walking point again and my point man was moving very slowly. The terrain was terrible and he was wary of going on the trail because of all the recent ambushes. We knew the enemy was all around us.

We were off trail and the brush was so thick we had to use machetes to cut through the jungle. Captain Workman asked me what was holding us up. He didn't like the slow pace and asked me how many enemies were in front of us. I told him that it felt like we were walking into an ambush. I didn't see anyone, nor did anyone else, but he kept prodding me.

The rule at that time was that we couldn't call in an air strike unless we had contact with the enemy or we spotted them. Budget cuts from Congress made funds tighter and air strikes were expensive.

Plus, Nixon had begun reducing troop levels and replacement soldiers were hard to come by. Looking back, I wonder how the tightening of the budget affected our ability to get all the help we needed, and how many lives it cost.

I was twenty years old and a little naive, but finally I caught on and said, "Oh yeah, they are just up ahead." The air strikes were called in and the Navy sent in the jets with napalm. Captain Workman knew that we weren't sure about the enemy, but he was the kind of leader who would support his men.

Before the jets, a spotter plane would fly in to identify the target areas by dropping a white phosphorous bomb. The spotter planes were small, slow moving propeller planes and the pilots had guts. They usually flew high enough, about 1,500 feet, to avoid the range of small arms fire, but could be hit with longer range missiles or anti-aircraft weapons. In order to remain nimble, they only wore their chicken plates, or flak vests, for protection. The Forward Air Controller (FAC) dropped red smoke grenades to mark the area the jets start to fire or drop bombs, and yellow for when to pull out.

The FACs were the only ones allowed to call in the air strikes to avoid miscommunication that could result in even greater casualties due to friendly fire. Once he marked the spot he got out of the way and a jet moving around 1800 mph flew in to drop the bombs. The jet pilot got near the target and slowed up a little and then 500 pound bombs rolled out of the bottom of these jets toward the targets. At this point, the bombs are moving faster than the plane so the pilot hit their afterburner and guns it out of there.

A few seconds later, the target was hit and the napalm exploded. Napalm is gasoline mixed with a jello substance. It either burns what it hits or it sucks all the oxygen from wherever it lands and kills either way. It is really impressive to watch.

Workman knew that he needed to call in the air strikes for us. We had been getting our asses kicked and we needed help. This assisted us greatly as it really cleared the jungle out in this area. We called in more artillery support for our operation.

Our air support greatly aided our work on the ground and, without it, we would have experienced a higher number of casualties. In addition to Marine aircraft based in Da Nang, we also received Navy aircraft support from carriers in the Gulf, and B-52 bombers that were stationed in Thailand and Guam. The Air Force encountered enemy aircraft resistance when bombing North Vietnam. There were dogfights with North Vietnamese pilots manning Russian and Chinese MiGs. A number of American pilots were shot down and held prisoners for years.

Even though the Americans owned the sky with our firepower those of us on the ground were still cautious when we heard airplanes flying overhead. Since we were so near the DMZ, those planes could be MiGs flown by the North Vietnamese. This was just another cautionary issue to worry about.

I took my squad for a patrol after the burn and we found remnants of the enemy. One time, we saw blood on the trail and followed it and saw a former NVA soldier splattered on a tree. The Vietnamese didn't bleed a lot because of their diet and small stature. If we saw some blood there was a good chance they were in pretty bad shape. By contrast, GIs bled like stuffed pigs.

Going on patrol the next few days was touch and go. We seemed to be losing soldiers every day. Heat stroke took a few guys, and we had to bring in choppers to get them out of there.

One assignment my squad had during this time was to retrieve a body from 1st platoon, a lieutenant, their platoon leader. I took about four or five of my squad to the next little ridge about a hundred yards away. I walked point over to them as I could sense that nobody wanted to move. The atmosphere was bad. In a week, we had lost two of the three platoon leaders and when we got to the platoon, they were pretty shook up.

The lieutenant was lying there, having just been hit with a RPG (rocket propelled grenade). His shirt was off and there were just two little marks above his heart. I couldn't believe those two little marks killed him but they said he dropped right away. He had a wife and young children and recently learned that his wife just had a baby. I knew that his family was going to be devastated.

We wrapped him in a poncho and started moving him through a narrow trail to an open area. We had to get him on a chopper in order to fly his body home. Finally, we got to an open area and the chopper was coming in. It was a LOH, Light Observation Helicopter, but we called it a Loach. It was smaller than the regular Huey we were all familiar with. It had a pilot and copilot and miniguns on the side with a small back seat, and that is where they wanted us to put the lieutenant.

I wanted this done quickly because once the enemy sees a chopper land, it zeros in because they know there will be GIs around. The chopper was hovering about four feet off the ground and we were trying to put our fallen soldier in it but he kept falling out. The chopper was tilting back and forth, time was ticking away, and I felt that we were going to get enemy fire in another couple of minutes.

Three or four guys were trying to get the body on the chopper with no success. I hopped on the chopper runners, tilting it even more. I pushed with my head and shoulders until I wedged the body in and the pilot felt he was secured. I stared at the body as the pilot took off. Then, we moved out of the area so the enemy wouldn't drop mortars in on us.

At this point, Captain Workman decided to combine all of us and move as one big platoon. Lt. Deuschle and Captain Workman were the only commissioned officers remaining. They were great to work for and, at this time, they had a hell of a job ahead of them.

We were running patrols to check out the area all of the time. One morning, two squads were sent out, one to the north and the other to the south. They were to go out fifty to a hundred yards, turn right and work their way back. Unfortunately, one turned right and the other turned left so they headed towards each other and they started shooting for a few minutes before we got them to stop. Nobody got hurt. We were glad because it could have been another ugly chapter to this operation. Of course, we kidded the guys about their shooting ability.

The morning of May 14th started out with one of the squads making contact with the enemy. We were now just one platoon and the action wasn't very far away. A couple men, Scofield and Wells were hit with small arms fire and an RPG, and we had to bring in a medevac chopper to get them out.

I got a call on my radio from Captain Workman. My RTO Edd Forrester was relaying my calls since I couldn't hear a thing over the radio after losing my hearing while shooting the machine gun on FSB Maureen. Captain Workman wanted to clear the area so we could safely bring in a chopper. He ordered an on-line sweep of the enemy bunker complex, that is, one line of soldiers all moving toward a target. You've seen this maneuver when watching a Civil War movie. Edd reassured me we had to do it, and we had to do it quickly to get the wounded out.

I spread out the squad of about fifteen men in a long line covering about forty yards across this little valley. It was dangerous in the jungle because we had to stay in line so nobody would get too far in front of each other. If a GI took a shot to either side in the thick jungle he might shoot a buddy in the back.

We traded fire earlier with the enemy and it was clear that they were well established. If we tried to sneak up in front of them, all they had to do was point their rifle at us and fire. I ran from one end of the squad to the other and, while on the move, I threw a lot of grenades. I kept the men on-line so nobody got behind.

When throwing a grenade, we pulled the pin and had five seconds until it exploded. If it exploded near us, we were dead. But, if we threw it in a bunker too soon, the enemy could pick it up and throw it back, and again we were dead. Since our enemy was in a bunker complex that we had to move through, our only option was to crawl up on them and toss grenades into their bunkers to secure them. To get to them, I crawled up and around so I could get close enough to toss in the grenades. They were built very solid, so I crawled on the top of them. I didn't know if my guys were still shooting in that direction. I worried about friendly fire, but I knew that we had to take out those bunkers.

When I was in position, I prepared to throw my grenades using what we called a "cook off." I pulled the pin and then I counted two or three seconds and then threw it so it goes off right away with no chance of it coming back out. When it went off, it shook me a little.

We had quite a few bunkers to clear and explosions were going off all over the place. I had taken out about four bunkers when I climbed on the top of another one. I remained on top for the first four, but for an unknown reason, after I threw the grenade in the bunker, I rolled off to the side of this one.

The grenade exploded and then there was a secondary explosion. The bunker must have had stored ammo. The explosion flipped me over and I thought all I had to worry about was the concussion just like after the others. But then I felt a twinge in my right ankle. Something happened but I wasn't sure what. It felt like I had been hit with a baseball bat. There was a little hole in my boot over the bone that sticks out.

We had cleared all the bunkers and we heard the choppers were on their way to take out the two wounded guys. Edd said the captain was on the radio and wanted to know what happened. I told him I was hit and it felt like a badly sprained ankle. Captain Workman was hoping I could continue because we had lost so many guys in recent days. I said that if I lightened my rucksack I should be able to keep going. The medic came over and took off my boot and saw that my ankle was about twice its normal size.

He told Workman that I had to go out on the chopper. I felt bad that I had to leave but I also knew if I stayed I was going to be a burden to the other guys. A few minutes before, I had been helping clear the way for the chopper to take out Schofield and Wells who were hit earlier, but now I was one of them to go. There was no LZ so the chopper had to hover over us and drop a cable with a little seat on it called a "Jungle Penetrator." They pulled Wells and Schofield up simultaneously and it seemed to take a long time.

We had just been in contact with the enemy so we knew they were all around, and a helicopter hovering fifty feet over our head was pretty noisy. I got on the seat and they started to haul me up. I remember waving to the guys, but I made myself as small as possible so the enemy had a tiny target. I heard of a guy waving as he was leaving on a chopper and he was shot in the belly.

Lifting me up seemed to take forever. I was signaling for them to take off as I had such a tight grip on that cable that I bet my finger prints are still on it. Finally they pulled me into the chopper and then they took off. From the time I was wounded to the time I was in the chopper was about thirty minutes and on my way to the hospital. I was impressed.

I felt a little guilty about leaving at that time. The wound was serious enough to be medevaced out, but I still felt that I let down my squad. Later, I talked with some of the guys and they said the next couple weeks were constant battles and they lost men every day. They estimated that they lost about forty percent from the original number of men. John Fraser told me that as bad as it was before I left, it got even worse later.

The pilots on choppers have greatly aided the fighting men by medevacing them from injury to treatment, on average, within an hour. In previous wars, many soldiers died from the same injuries that occurred during the Vietnam Conflict.

Chopper pilots risked their lives inserting themselves under enemy fire to bring troops in or take them out. There were numerous occasions when the gun ships were so vitally important in keeping us safe. When we heard the sound of choppers, we knew they were our guys.

Helicopter pilots had the highest risk job in Vietnam after the infantry. Due to a shortage of helicopter pilots, the Army opened up a pilot program that allowed non-officers to become helicopter pilots through the Warrant Officer program. Given the thousands of sorties flown, (sorties are defined as when the engine was turned on and when it was turned off) their success rate was remarkable. Those of us in combat literally owe our lives to the bravery and skills of helicopter pilots.

Edd Forrestor – RTO

Tisch, Fraser, Nelson, Me

Nice view of mountains

Impact of Napalm

Chapter Seven

Don's Recovery

I was medevaced by helicopter to the 85th Evacuation Unit, which was pretty much like the TV show MASH. I got off the chopper before lunch. My leg was broken at the ankle, the tibia, so I was able to hop from the landing pad to the hospital fifty yards away. The medics were running to get all of us but I went on my own as Wells had eye injuries and his were more serious than mine.

I was uncertain about my fitness and the future of continuing to fight. Some guys who were medevaced out were patched up and then sent back into battle, whereas others were never heard from again, presumably shipped back to the states.

They took us right in and the nurses started getting us ready to see the doctors. I sat on the floor next to the exam table where a guy had a bullet or shrapnel in his right shoulder. The doctor started cutting all the flesh right down to the bone and it was bright white. He explained that he took out anything that might cause the risk of infection. Well, I looked down at my swollen ankle and it was about three times the size of a normal ankle. I thought that I'm just a skinny little kid and if they cut that kind of flesh from me, hell, I won't have an ankle left.

So when that guy was done he said to me, "Hop up, your next." I thought "bullshit." I tried to stall and think of a better idea, but I didn't. I hopped on the table and he started digging around for the metal that was located in the center of my ankle in the bone that sticks out.

They gave me a local anesthetic or I would still be in prison for killing the doctor. The doctor explained everything he was doing and I just sat there with a ring-side seat to a little surgery. The entire operation reminded me of MASH, when it was good with Wayne Rogers and Mclean Stevens. The doctors wore the same uniform that I was wearing, and they had a great sense of humor. Finally, he said he could not get the metal out and he didn't want to tear up my ankle anymore.

At this point the hole was about the size of a quarter and deep. I stayed that night in a hospital and received lots of medications, mostly penicillin and morphine.

The next day they loaded me onto a C-130 and flew me to Cam Ranh Bay in the southern part of Vietnam. The C-130 is a workhorse plane that hauls just about everything. They stacked us wounded four or five high on the side walls of the plane. The week I was wounded the body count was 101 dead and about 900 wounded, so the hospitals were very busy.

The Cam Ranh Bay hospital could handle more serious problems than the 85th Evacuation Unit. They did the best they could, but they too were limited. The doctors reviewed my injuries to determine how severely I was hurt. There were four of us to a room and the doctor came in to decide whether the surgery could be done there, or if they would ship us out to Japan.

He signed off on my going to Japan and once that happens, I would not return to battle another day. As I recall, they shipped all four of us to Japan. Some guys had limbs missing and were pretty banged up. I felt pretty lucky, by comparison.

While still in Cam Ranh Bay hospital, I was in contact with the Red Cross people and I asked them if they could locate my brother Mark in Pleiku. They were able to get the number and when I called, I got one of the clerks on the phone who knew him. He said that Mark was walking toward the office. Unknown to me at the time, he was just returning from a thirty day leave back home and was trying to get me out of the field.

While talking on the phone, we had to use the word "over" or "stop" when we finished talking while releasing the "talk button."

"Mark, is that you, over?"

"Yes it is, over."

"This is Don. I got hit and I am in Cam Ranh Bay, and I will be shipped to Japan, over."

"Are you going to be sent back in the field, over?"

"Once I am sent to Japan, I won't be coming back."

"Well, good luck to you. I'll see you back home, over."

We were flown to Japan in a big hospital plane. The nurses were real troopers and they took good care of us during the six-hour trip. In Japan, I had surgery on the ankle. Back then, they experimented with different procedures. In preparation for my surgery, they gave me a spinal tap and it ended up about as bizarre as the movie. For surgery, I was naked except for the stylish looking hairnet. They rolled me over and told me to curl into the fetal position and then started to insert the needle in my lower spine. It started to crunch as it was going in.

It hurt badly and I said, "Hell with this," and I hopped off the operating table. I was butt naked. I'm sure I scared the doctors as they backed up as I tried to get the hell out of there. They were yelling "Catch him." When naked with a broken leg, I wasn't going too far too fast. When they finally captured me, they put me back on the table and continued with the surgery. Regrettably, it ended with the same result of not being able to extract the shrapnel. I'm sure that doctor is at some country club talking about this one naked, crazy guy who jumped off the table during surgery and started running.

During my two week stay, I was recovering and getting around in my wheelchair, able to eat warm food and not C-rations. I went to the movies with other guys, wheeling ourselves to the theatre. Since there were so many guys in wheel chairs, they ripped out half the seats and put two-by-fours on the floor. We parked our wheelchairs and sat there and watched the movie. Pretty cool, huh.

After a couple weeks they sent me back to the U.S. for more surgery. They located a hospital that could handle my unique problem and was also close to my home. The closest was Valley Forge, Pennsylvania and it handled many different injuries including leg problems. Other hospitals handled severe injuries like burns, eyes, arms, etc. When I landed at the hospital by helicopter from the airport, a couple of firemen assigned to the landing pad for safety waved and welcomed me home. I don't know why I remember this, but I do.

I met with a doctor and he said he would simply remove the metal and it would heal with minimal problems so I was feeling pretty good. But there was a big earthquake in Peru, and my doctor was sent to help out for about three weeks. They put my surgery on hold, so I kept rehabbing and waited. The medics came to our hospital beds every morning to change the dressings on our wounds. They poured peroxide in the hole and scrubbed my wound with a long Q-tip.

Initially, they did this two times a day to prevent infection. The medic was real busy with more serious injuries as my roommates had missing limbs and they needed more care than me. I had him park his medical cart by me and I did all the work myself. Later, they determined that scrubbing an open wound with peroxide was not the best way for it to heal.

During my recovery and rehabilitation, I was only able to take six-inch steps walking down the hall. The first few times I walked, my ankle swelled up, but I knew that the more I walked the sooner and better my recovery would be. I was motivated to walk as those who could were invited by the Salvation Army to a baseball game at old Connie Mack Stadium in Philadelphia, the last year it was in play. About forty of us went by bus to a game with pretty good seats. They bought us beer and hot dogs and treated us great. There was a big crowd and we sat there in our blue pajamas and the crowd ignored us. Nobody booed us, which we felt was a plus. I am thankful to the Salvation Army, and I faithfully give to their charity drives.

When my doctor returned from Peru, he looked at the ankle and thought he would do more damage if he did the surgery as the hole in my ankle was filling in. He figured leaving a couple pieces of metal in me wouldn't be so bad, so I still have my metal souvenirs of Vietnam in my ankle. I was disappointed that I was unable to gain full recovery and it would come back to haunt me in later years.

During rehab, I read the daily military newspaper, *Stars and Stripes*, and each Thursday they released the names of the dead for that week. I met a lot of guys in infantry over the past year and it seemed that I knew at least one person each week that died. I quit reading the paper. I read that Captain Don Workman was killed on July 21, 1970 when the fifth chopper that was extracting the D/1-506th was hit by AK-47 fire and the chopper rolled over and killed him. He was awarded the Silver Star posthumously.

Captain Workman's story and the final big battles in Vietnam are detailed in the book, *Ripcord* by Keith Nolan. FSB Maureen was part of a February to July build up of pivotal battles that decided the outcome of the war. Many have said that we won all the battles, but lost the war. But, in July, we lost the battle at Ripcord. "The ordeal of Ripcord expressed the ultimate frustration of the Vietnam War: The inability of the American military to bring the resources to win on the battlefield." *Ripcord.*

After a couple months at Valley Forge, I was reassigned to a base closer to home, Ft. Knox near Louisville, Ky. In the summer of 1970, I had about eight months of duty left to serve. My job was to train South Vietnamese officers in combat procedures of a mechanized unit which consisted of APC (Armored Personnel Carriers) and tanks. Since I had been trained as an infantryman, this was quite an adjustment as I had never worked with any of this equipment before. Most of us at Ft. Knox were Vietnam veterans. In fact, Schofield from 2nd platoon was with me. He was one of the guys taken out on the chopper the same day as me.

I spent my remaining months there and applied for an early out so I could attend college and get on with my life. Meanwhile, Mark was still in Vietnam serving his remaining months.

191

Part Three

Epilogue

A Trip Over & Freedom Bird Home

Chapter Eight

Mark's Extended Tour

I got a thirty-day leave and came home to visit the family and friends. However, events unfolded that I would never have anticipated. After arriving in Ashtabula, I discovered that my car was sold while I was away, perhaps thinking I wouldn't return.

I visited Wally McArthur, the golf professional at the ACC, whom I had worked for a couple years prior to getting drafted. Wally was nice to let me use his second car on some occasions. I'm sure I abused that privilege, but I was very grateful.

While walking through Carlisle's department store, I met Vicky Carlisle. Vicky and I hit it off and we started dating and spent much of my leave together. She is a very pretty girl with a great sense of humor.

My friend Jim Nyland called about 4 a.m., on April 24, 1970, and said his son Mark was born. I drove to Gallipolis, his wife's home town in southeast Ohio on the Ohio River. It is the home of Bob Evans Farms (famous for its sausage and restaurants with home cooked meals and superb biscuits). While visiting his wife Ann in the hospital, Jim and I probed the merits of circumcision until she abruptly cut off the discussion.

During my leave, unrest on college campuses was heating up. There had been campus demonstrations following Nixon's April 30, 1970 bombing of Cambodia. In addition, Nixon authorized several thousands of ARVN and U.S. troops to invade Cambodia and to ward off the communists, the Khmer Rouge.

A riot ensued at Kent State, and the ROTC building was burned down with some injuries. Governor James Rhodes called in the National Guard on Saturday, May 2, even though the local police thought they could handle the situation. Due to a miscommunication, the National Guard did not receive the order to leave the campus. They had been on drills the previous weekend.

My older brother Pat was attending Kent State, located about ninety minutes from Ashtabula. On Sunday, I drove him to college so I could use his car during the week. On Monday May 4, 1970, following a weekend with virtually no sleep for the guardsmen, demonstrations continued.

The National Guard was ordered to throw tear gas, but a single "warning" shot was fired. The Guardsmen opened fire resulting in four deaths and nine others wounded, one paralyzed. One of the killed was an ROTC cadet walking to class. A couple days later on Wednesday, May 6, school was called off for the year and I picked up my brother. This was not an isolated incident. The National Guard was called out to calm uprising in twenty-eight different confrontations throughout the country.

Nearly twenty percent of all colleges in the U.S. cancelled the remainder of the year, affecting about four million students. Although tragic, this was a watershed moment as it was clear that something had to be done to wind down the war quickly.

The U.S. Senate stepped in and demanded that all troops be pulled from Cambodia and bombings stopped. Further, they passed a resolution denying military funds for use in Laos. Later, Congress repealed the Gulf of Tonkin resolution, thus limiting the president's use of power in that region.

I was reluctant to head back to Vietnam, but my thirty-day leave ended. I called the Red Cross to get an extension for some bogus reason, but it was denied. I then made my flight plans. I flew to San Francisco and had secured an Air Force flight to Ft. Lewis later that evening. I spent a couple hours with Susie Hill, a high school friend, and her roommate. She was kind enough to cancel her date and took me to Chinatown and we rode the trolley cars and stopped for a drink.

Later, they took me across the Golden Gate Bridge to Oakland so I could catch my flight, but it was cancelled. We drove back to her apartment where I slept for a couple hours before they took me to the San Francisco airport where I took a commercial flight, wearing my uniform to get a military discount.

Upon arrival at Ft. Lewis, my orders showed that I was late in returning so they put me in a holding cell with other guys for a couple hours. After they verified that I had called the Red Cross, and I was crazy enough to volunteer to go back to Vietnam, they let me go.

While waiting for my flight to be scheduled, I read the Sunday newspaper. There was an article about Jonathan Winters, the great comedian, explaining why he had a nervous breakdown in the past year. He said he would sign up for an engagement in Las Vegas and then he was so successful they wanted him to take his show to New York, L.A. and Chicago. "Then, they want you in Atlanta, Detroit, Dallas and Cleveland. The next thing you know, you wind up in Ashtabula."

As I was flying back to Vietnam for my second tour, I wondered if I had made a mistake. Even though I only had about six months left, I was still concerned that I was pushing the envelope. After arriving in Pleiku, I was surprised when my ride picked me up wearing a flak vest, helmet and a weapon. From the day I left, they had incoming rockets, and got up at five every morning to sit in the bunkers until daylight. Further, we had to maintain a safe distance from each other when walking outside and were to stand about fifteen feet apart from others in the mess hall line. Some guys treated my leave as an omen and they didn't want me leaving any time soon. I still had six months to serve and only had an R&R remaining.

During my leave, I learned that my brother Don was in Vietnam as an infantryman. When I arrived back in Pleiku, I immediately talked with Warrant Officer Ives and said that I wanted to request a transfer for my brother to come and work in our supply room. The Army's rule would allow us to be stationed together.

Ives said we could take care of that but he needed me to go that day to our company located in An Khe as they were missing a lot of supplies. Captain Edwards served in battalion headquarters but he volunteered to serve another six months to get command time, a necessary requirement to garner promotions. I took the next chopper out to An Khe and arrived in about an hour, hoping to spend the day and get back to headquarters. Captain Edwards said that he took inventory when he assumed command and found a number of items missing and needed my help. He was appreciative of my being there and even had me sleep in the officer's quarters.

I interviewed the supply sergeant who had been there awhile, but he was not in charge. When I assured him that I was not out to get him, he was more helpful. Some guy took a two-and-a-half ton truck to Saigon and then went home, just leaving it in the airport parking lot. A generator that could light up a village was in fact lighting up a village about a mile down the road. This $50,000 generator was sold for $500 by a guy who needed money. A jeep, weapons, ammunition, clothes, sheets, and eating utensils were missing. In short, this company was a real mess, or "in a world of hurt," as we said.

In the next couple days, we recreated documents to show proper disposition and requisitioned replacement items. I agreed to send a bunch of stuff on the next chopper. Unfortunately, when it was time for me to go, the choppers were grounded because of weather, and convoys were delayed as well due to heavy gun fire and ambushes on the roads.

In all, I spent about five days there instead of the expected one-to-two day turnaround. I eventually hitched a ride on a convoy, keeping a sharp eye for a potential ambush. I was deeply impressed with the beautiful countryside and envisioned golf courses and resorts dotting the landscape in the future.

I was literally walking toward my office building when someone called out to me and said my brother was on the phone. During our exchange, he explained that he got hit and was on his way to Japan, and then back to the states for further recovery.

In his quest to clean up the company, Captain Edwards took action to reduce the amount of drugs while attempting to bring the soldiers in line. When some guys didn't like a policy, they sent a warning by rolling a grenade into a room with the pin in it. The implication was that the next time, the pin would be pulled. This initiative was called "fragging"-- when an officer or NCO was targeted by his troops.

Captain Edwards

It was named after the weapon of choice, the fragmentation grenade. This practice became more widespread as the frustration with the war and leaders escalated and drugs became more prominent. The number of fraggings increased as the war continued and there were about 800 incidents with eighty-five associated deaths.

Captain Edwards was not easily intimidated. He continued to press his agenda for cleaning up the operation and getting rid of drugs. However, a short time later, someone shot an anti-tank weapon at him but, fortunately, it hit a four–by-six foundation piece of wood and shattered rather than Edwards taking a direct hit. Regrettably, Captain Edwards got shrapnel in his eyes and he was medevaced out of the country for treatment. I can only hope that he fully recovered from his injury and was able to live a full life as he was a great guy and a good leader.

During my 30-day leave, the MACV movie theater took a direct hit with a rocket and there was nothing left. Over the next couple weeks, there was no further enemy activity so schedules and attire went back to normal.

In mid-1970, many guys that completed their tour were not replaced. Now, we were down to about a half-a-dozen guys and reducing every month. The number of guys in the motor pool, generator shop, and the field units also declined.

It was clear that the war was winding down, at least for us. We were running out of work, and there was little for us to do during the day. We had time to practice and play softball during the summer. In the early fall of 1970, we played football. Some guys read novels during the work day, and others spent more time at the NCO club. I had taken over the dwindling team from Sergeant Wilson and CW2 Ives who rotated out.

The 4th Infantry Division moved from Camp Enari to Camp Radcliffe near An Khe and was then deactivated by the end of 1970. We thought we might be overrun without the infantry protection. Thankfully, it didn't happen.

Although negotiations were thwarted by both the South and the North Vietnamese, troop levels continued to decline.

We often talked about who was going to be left to lock the gate and turn out the lights.

Sydney R&R

I wasn't sure where I would go for my next R&R, but Bill Burkhart was leaning toward Sydney, Australia. I figured that I was less likely to ever visit it compared to Hawaii, my other strong choice. The downside was that it was June and that meant winter months in Sydney with moderate temperatures. Surely we would not see the bikini clad women on the beautiful beaches shown in the brochure.

Leaving Saigon, we flew four hours into Darwin in the north of Australia, where the plane was sprayed and our shoes were vacuumed to ensure we didn't bring any disease into the country. We then flew another four hours to Sydney where we deplaned and were ushered into the reception center. There, Bill and I met a woman in her thirties, Lilly Wolf. Since we were older than other GIs, she recommended some places that would be more suitable for us. She helped arrange for nice hotel accommodations for $10 a day. We gave her our names and she called later and arranged to meet.

Mark, Lil & kids in Sydney

The unique Kings Cross area was the local hot spot for Australians with its small shops, restaurants and night clubs. However, since the American GIs became more dominant, the hookers and con-men moved in and the locals went elsewhere.

The first night we saw "HAIR." The next day we rented some clubs and played golf at Moore Park Golf course that wasn't in very good shape. One afternoon, Lil and her two children, Jerry and Ronny, ages nine and six respectively, took us for a tour of the city with its red roofs, and to notable spots. We took a ferry ride to the zoo, passing by the now famous music hall that was under construction with local debate about the delay and increasing costs. The zoo was memorable as the koala bears sat in the trees drugged from eating eucalyptus tree leaves all day.

We attended parties sponsored by local residents, mostly English people. One couple had escaped from Russia when they were teenagers, crawling under barbed wire, but were now married with two daughters. I tasted caviar for the first and only time—it was underwhelming.

Bill and I had lunch on the 47th floor of a circular restaurant that rotated so we could see the entire city in about an hour. The buffet cost about $3 and, although Bill was reluctant to spend that kind of money, he eventually gave in. We enjoyed Viva Music, a chamber group after dinner at Mama Mia's, an Italian restaurant.

Sydney Symphony Hall

Sydney was the longest of all the R&R locations, and we started to run out of things to do. I told Bill that if we had another day, I was going to get a part time job. A day later, we headed back to Vietnam.

Short Timer

During the summer of 1970, I sent letters detailing my time in Vietnam to Vicky who was traveling Europe. I had her itinerary so I sent letters for her to receive at her next location. I carefully worded the letters because if there was any misunderstanding it would take six weeks and several letters to explain the true meaning of a comment.

A short timers' calendar was a 30- to 60-day calendar and we checked off each day showing how many days were left to serve in Vietnam. Although it was a reminder of how long we had to serve, it was also a daily reminder of a possible twist of fate. We had all experienced at least one story of a wayward mortar or rocket landing near us. We thought our enemy was poor shots, but they were due to get one right in on us. Near the end, I would lie in my bunk at night and wonder if an errant rocket might hit me.

I was approached about reenlisting. I would receive a tax free payment of $10,000 for another six years. Figuring this was only about $1,600 a year, I thought I could do better outside the service. Lieutenant Queen wanted to remain in the military but since he was OCS, he worried that there would be a reduction in force, or RIF.

Serving my full three years of active duty would have kept me in the service until March 18, 1971. However, when returning from an overseas assignment with less than five months to serve, the Army gives an Early Separation of Overseas Returnee, or a "150 day drop." On 20 October 1970, I left for Saigon, transferred to Japan, and then flew for nine and a half hours on my "freedom bird," straight into Oakland, the departure point for many leaving the service.

While processing the termination of my service, I was paid for any unused leave and final pay. We were cautioned to safeguard our cash and valuables, amounting to several hundred dollars. Another guy and I watched for each other as we showered and dressed. Throughout the service, we guarded our wallet by putting it under our pillow to avoid theft.

Thus, I only served two years, seven months and three days. That is, if I was counting. I saw a lot of the U.S. and parts of the world that I would never have seen without the benefit of my time in the military. I made it through without a scratch, or the clap.

Although my active duty was completed, I was obligated up to six years in active reserve or in an emergency until March 1974. The local reserve unit didn't need my MOS and didn't need me.

Colonel, Mark Bronze Star

I received my Honorable Discharge on March 12, 1974. My DD-214, listed the awards I received during my service.

National Defense Service Medal

Vietnam Service Medal

Vietnam Campaign Medal

Army Commendation Medal

Good Conduct Medal

Bronze Star Medal

After being discharged for a year, Vietnam Veterans are requested to get a physical exam at a VA center to determine if there are any lingering diseases, exposure to Agent Orange, or any other infirmity. If you want to see the casualties of war, visit a VA hospital. After completing my physical exam, I walked out looking at the near blind, those with missing limbs and countless other problems. I passed through the exit doors, put my hand on the railing to steady myself, and wiped away my tears.

Chapter Nine

After the Army

We were let out of the Army in late 1970. Like many Vietnam veterans, we simply wanted to move on and live our lives. We had much more we wanted to accomplish. It was a relief that we had made our commitment to the military and would not have to confront that issue when seeking employment. On the other hand, some employers felt that Vietnam veterans were unstable and were unwilling to hire them. Since we were both going back to school and were seeking our former jobs, or jobs with those friendly to veterans, we did not encounter any hostile treatment.

Mark Shaughnessy

When it was all over, I was warmly received home, especially from my family and friends. I never encountered any poor treatment from others. Perhaps my being six feet tall, in good shape and a scowl on my face had something to do with it. I never understood why anyone would ridicule those who served their country, no matter how controversial the issue. They didn't really have much choice.

I visited Vicky Carlisle in Boston where she was attending the Katie Gibbs School. While walking down the street I doubled over in pain from eating too much rich food after leaving the Army. I changed to a bland diet and immediately improved. Don't change habits!

I received a letter from my Vietnam laundry girl, Lam, in November asking for candy and thanking me for getting her soap. Dong, the girl I helped get paid, also said hello to "number ten" on the first floor. She said the 43rd Signal Battalion was going with the 71st Evacuation Unit.

Vicky and I got engaged during Christmas 1970, but we called it off about six months later. People asked why I wouldn't marry into one of the richest families in Northeast Ohio. I said I didn't want to work Friday nights at the department store. Vicky and I exchanged a lot of letters during my final six months in Vietnam and they would have been a great reference for this narrative but, in her period of despair after our breakup, she burned them.

I gave my mother two weeks to give away the ill fitting clothes from Hong Kong to her church friends or I was giving them to Goodwill.

Dick Huhta and I got together and he showed me more than 2,000 slides and explained how so many guys in his unit were either killed or severely injured. I remarked that he was telling me about nearly everyone in his company. He shrugged and said that is the way it was. Dick became the radio man in his unit, which is the first target of the enemy in an ambush. The enemy wants to prevent the RTO from calling in to get reinforcements, artillery support or helicopters to strafe the enemy.

He said that his time in Vietnam was the best of times and the worst of times. While the fighting was scary, it was also exhilarating. He recalled the enemy walking in mortars on his location, and the times he strapped himself to a tree at night to get some sleep without sliding into water and drowning. Dick said that he probably should have been killed a number of times but he was simply lucky.

Steve Grippi went into the FBI upon completion of his tour in Vietnam and retired a couple years ago.

Don and I returned to Kent State in first quarter, 1971, rooming together in a trailer. Although we were both just out of the Army, we rarely talked about our time in the military.

I completed my final five quarters at Kent State University and graduated with a B.S. in Business Management in June 1972. I was paid $175 a month from the G.I. Bill and deeply appreciated that program. I enjoyed the final year and a half in college, being able to take courses and go to the library to study without having to go to work every day.

In my final quarter, I worked as the assistant golf professional at the ACC and had to pack my final courses into a couple days. My schedule dictated that I take a professor who had a reputation for being tough. The course applied knowledge of marketing, management, accounting and finance on case studies. I did very well in the course and he pulled me aside to encourage me to get an MBA. I gave it some thought and also considered law school, but I was twenty-eight, running out of savings, and was ready to move on. To what, I didn't know. I worked at the country club for the summers of 1971 and 1972.

During the winter of 1973, Wally McArthur had resigned, and I was asked to interview for the head pro position at the ACC. The nephew of one of the members got the job, but only lasted one year. Later, the fellow who interviewed me admitted to the former pro, Red Lathrop, that they had made a mistake and should have hired me. That was gratifying.

A friend of my mother, Frank Starkey, an insurance salesman who also sold me my first insurance policy, put my name in for a position with Prudential. It was as a field auditor that reviewed salesmen's books and office procedures to ensure against theft. I was hired for about $8,500 a year; good money compared to recent earnings and there were benefits.

Mother Louise was a wonderful person, and a friend to everyone she met. I recall many Friday nights when I came home from work and we watched "The Odd Couple" and "The Rockford Files" while eating homemade popcorn with lots of butter, just the way she liked it. All of us boys and my sister truly loved this woman and knew how important she was, especially for what she did for us after our dad died.

Todd Crandall, a good friend and golfer who played for Florida State, and I took Louise and her friend Betty Kelleher to a Cleveland Indians game. We picked one of the busiest nights, when Gaylord Perry pitched his last game for the Indians. They were thrilled, but not as much as I was to see their joy.

Louise also had a lot of fun and would often laugh so hard in trying to tell a funny story that she couldn't finish it. My mother got dressed up for Halloween to go trick or treating and one year, she dressed up in biker clothes with a leather jacket and helmet, and nobody recognized her.

On July 13, 1975, Mom died. Some said it was the largest visiting crowd to the funeral home they had ever seen. At the service, the priest reminded us that she was a faithful follower. He said she told the priest after a lengthy sermon that she missed the beginning of "All in the Family," one of her favorite television shows, and she would appreciate him keeping to his normal schedule. Louise left us way too soon, but I am thankful for the time she was with us. I learned a lot of lessons from her. She was alive to see her children grow up, kind of. We miss her a lot, and often.

Brother Pat was a smoker, about three packs a day from high school and beyond for the next forty years. Over the years, Pat, my brother Jim, and brother-in-law George would give each other a carton of cigarettes for Christmas. Although it seemed humorous at the time, eventually they all suffered from their smoking habits. In the summer of 1997, Pat continued to smoke even though he was on a respirator. A couple weeks after we visited him he died, not able to get to his oxygen. Unfortunately, my brother-in-law also passed away a couple years later from cancer, even though he quit smoking years earlier. My brother Jim, who served in the Army in Hawaii, is now retired but he too suffers from smoking, but is doing well.

I've been fortunate to marry a loving wife. Lisa is attractive, smart and artistic. She is from Waverly Hall, a small town near Columbus, Ga. She has a major in accounting and a minor in music from Brenau College in North Georgia.

She plays piano and sings very well, but not as often as I would like. We met in Atlanta, moved to Houston right after getting married in 1984, transferred to Oklahoma City in 1985, and had our first child Lannie soon after. We moved back to Atlanta in 1987 and our second daughter Lindsay was born in 1989. We have remained in Atlanta for the duration with one exception. We moved to Florida in 2000, but Lisa and the kids missed their friends so we moved back to Atlanta.

There have been many who have influenced my life. Walter "Red" Lathrop and his wife Eunie made it to age eighty before they passed away. I visited them about every ten years or so and they had a very good life. Regrettably, their son and my friend George, who introduced me to Bob Dylan's music, died just a couple years ago. I saw him just before his passing and we reconnected as if there wasn't thirty years since we had seen each other.

I also got reacquainted with Ted Peters, Red's half brother, in Clearwater, when I worked in Florida in 2000-2003. He is of Ted Peters Smoked Fish fame. Unfortunately, he was struck by a car and died.

In the late '90s, as I was driving from Greensboro, NC, to Atlanta on I-85, nearing Charlotte, I could feel a pain in my back right side, and it immediately took me back to my episode in Vietnam that Christmas day. I made it to a nearby emergency room where they diagnosed kidney stones and gave me some medication.

Jim Nyland and I have remained good friends. He served in the Army as a dentist at Ft. Jackson, South Carolina and remained in Columbia in private practice. During one visit, after Jim had divorced, he was starting to date. My daughter Lannie was petting one of his dogs when it reached back and bit her on the lip. Jim called Joel Sussman, a pediatrician friend, and he prescribed a topical medication. While at the pharmacy, I saw an attractive pharmacist that looked like a single woman. She didn't have that tired look of a married woman with children.

I told Jim about her and they connected and got married within a couple years and have a son Ben. Unfortunately, Jim has suffered as he lost his son, Scott, in a boating accident on a fishing vessel. His son Mark is married with a beautiful daughter and with Jill and Ben, it helps fill the void.

In April 2007, playing golf with my friend Peter Lehrman, we joined a man about 70 and a woman friend. He was in the Korean Army and served in Pleiku, Vietnam. He became head of the Asian movement of the Boy Scouts and had traveled the world, but I was the first person he met that served in Pleiku at the same time he was there. We became instant comrades and traded war stories during the round. He thanked the U.S. for keeping South Korea free during the Korean War.

My caddy mate, Dave Floor, and I are still good friends and we get together every couple years to relive some old memories and to create new ones. He has been married a long time to Judy and they have two girls with families of their own. He is a wonderful guy and I appreciate his friendship.

I worked in corporate America for more than thirty years, heading up sales and marketing departments for companies such as The Prudential, Blue Cross & Blue Shield of Georgia, Jefferson-Pilot and the Ceridian Corporation. I became a student of the sales and management process, reading or listening to over 200 books and tapes. I even provided a book of the month to my sales managers and sales reps to keep them abreast of current ideas.

Based on 30 years experience managing sales organizations, I wrote a book, *Sales Secrets*, a summary of the best ideas used by those successful in sales.

I have not visited the Vietnam Memorial in Washington, D.C. After nearly 40 years out of the service, I'm not sure I am up to it.

Don Shaughnessy

Discharge date was December 29, 1970 from Ft. Knox, Kentucky. I got an early discharge to return to college. I remember getting my final physical exam that day. A doctor pulled me aside and said, "Kid, I know you want to get out of here as fast as you can but you would be wise to fill out some papers." He told me that the metal in me was going to create problems for me in later years and I would need documentation to support my claims. To this day, I appreciate his good advice. I'm glad I listened to him because the VA didn't argue with me years later about my bad ankle and hearing problems.

Upon completion of military service, I worked at the Ashtabula Post Office for more than 30 years until I retired in 2004. I earned a Bachelor's degree from Kent State University. I reunited with my Gashouse Gang buddies and we played sports year round including softball, basketball, golf and now bocci. Since my retirement, I have stayed active in the Ashtabula community with the Elks Club, YMCA, and Speech and Hearing Organization, serving on their boards for a number of years.

I traveled to Washington D.C. for the opening day of the Vietnam Memorial in 1982. During my visit, I discovered that of the 58,000 deaths, more than 10,000 were from friendly fire. I drove in, studied the wall, turned around and drove home.

On May 5, 2007, I went to Fairfield, Illinois for a dedication of a memorial to honor Kenneth Kays, a recipient of the Medal of Honor for his actions at Fire Support Base Maureen. Kenneth Kays was a conscientious objector who went to Canada but then joined the Army when he was told that he wouldn't have to fight. Rather, he would be a medic helping others who saw action. As you may recall, Kays had a leg blown off helping others on FSB Maureen.

The ceremony included a Pledge of Allegiance and the National Anthem as well as the Presentation of Colors by local members of the VFW and the color guard from the 506th Regimental Combat Team, 101st Airborne Division from nearby Ft. Campbell. Three members of the 506th Infantry who served with Kays in Vietnam unveiled the memorial in his honor.

The Medal of Honor is given for outstanding service and bravery. There have been only nineteen recipients since WWII in the 101st Airborne Division. Kays was awarded the Medal of Honor by President Nixon. Ken had difficulty adjusting to life after Vietnam and died November 29, 1991, taking his own life.

During this visit to Fairfield, I reconnected with Greg Phillips who received the Silver Star, Ken David who was awarded the Distinguished Service Cross, and Steve "The Greek" Avgerinos earned the Bronze Star with "V" Device Citation. With what I now know about what the 2nd Platoon went through on Maureen that night, the acts of bravery from Greg, Ken and Steve were remarkable. I was unaware until then that the well deserved medals had been awarded.

The guys provided insight on the night when the 2nd platoon of D 1st of 506th was attacked. Their stories of bravery and that of Ken Kays are recounted in *Troubled Hero*, authored by Randy Mills about those that faced the onslaught on May 5, 1970 on FSB Maureen. Randy Mills called me in 2002 and wanted to know what I could tell him of the battle but I only remembered about ten minutes of it. I provided a picture I had taken of FSB Maureen and it was included in his book. I called John Fraser but he only recalled about five minutes of the battle. I was relieved that I wasn't the only one who forgot such an important event. After the war, I talked with John a few times and he was always a class act. Regrettably, John Fraser died in 2009.

I reconnected with Mel "Holly" Hollingsworth and he recovered from getting shot in the back on FSB Maureen and lives in Mississippi.

I recently spoke with Ed "Rebel" Deuschle, and he recounted some of the details that I have described. Landing on Firebase Maureen had a lasting impact on him. He made a pact with the Lord that if he got out of there alive he would devote his life to Him. Well, true to his word, he became a Baptist minister in Mississippi. He is now Dr. Ed Deuschle, Director of the Church Planting Department of the Mississippi Baptist Convention Board. Ed lives in Madison, Mississippi with his wife Rita.

Serving next to Ed Deuschle, John Fraser and Edd Forrester was fortunate for me. I was amazed at their bravery under adverse circumstances. Writing this book has allowed me the opportunity to make contact with a bunch of guys I respect the most.

There are many other great stories of guys who fought bravely in Vietnam and I have been fortunate to know some from Ashtabula. Because we experienced similar challenges, we are able to relate to the challenges each faced. Some of us are more willing to talk about the day-to-day experiences to better understand what happened as some days and battles became a blur to us.

A feeling of camaraderie among infantry soldiers remains to this day. It exists among Jack Lemmon, Mike Campbell, Monte Foltz, Joe St Angelo, Lanny Swiger and Dave Nicholas, all local Ashtabula guys that spent time in the field. Jack, Mike, Monte and I served in the 101st and we have this common bond that doesn't really need to be talked about, but it's there. I met Jack a few years after I returned from 'Nam and we worked at the Post Office together for years. He and Mike were there in 1969 and they say they cleared the way for me. Jack says, "Hey we were winning when I left. What the hell did you do?"

Dave Nicholas served in the 4th Infantry division. My friend Tim Palmer from Minnesota served in the Americal Division. Gino Platano, who played high school football for Edgewood against my brother Mark, served with the 173rd Airborne. Lanny and I worked at the post office together for many years.

Alan Pucci and Basile Dolbejeff, a.k.a. Joe Graham, were Harbor High graduates who served as door gunners on Huey choppers, and they both extended their tours in Vietnam.

Coming back from Vietnam was different from other wars. Vietnam Veterans were not treated warmly so I didn't make a big deal about being a veteran. I never put on my uniform for my friends. While hitchhiking home through Cleveland some guy was giving me a bunch of shit. I told him that I got drafted and to get off my back. No one ever spit on me. I just tried to blend back into normal society. I don't regret being in the military or going to Vietnam. I had experiences that I never could have imagined.

Some guys struggled with coming home and adjusting to everyday life. Their memories are tucked away while others relive their time, wondering what else they could have done to prevent injury or death to their fellow soldiers. In some instances, these memories cause painful side effects.

Meeting with a number of different veterans groups and talking with great guys has been very rewarding for me, even therapeutic. We are protective of each other and respect every person's contribution, regardless of our job in Vietnam. We enjoy the company and laugh at ourselves, trying to make light of our situation and the past. The alternative can put a drain on a person, and sometimes it does.

I witnessed soldiers accomplish many heroic acts saving others lives while putting their own in the line of fire. I saw too many good soldiers die. I have great respect for all who served and hope that those who are injured or suffer recurrent problems can achieve peace knowing that they did what their country asked of them. They did it with honor, and to the best of their abilities.

The VA continues to provide me treatment for war injuries to my ankle and for hearing loss. I applaud the efforts of the doctors at the VA who have been so helpful to me. I don't ask for any special benefits, but only that veterans of all wars receive the care that is necessary to provide them with a life free from pain, so they can live their life with dignity.

I have been fortunate to lead a fairly normal life, still dogged by pain, but otherwise I am fine. I married and have a wonderful daughter who is a lot of fun. I have a full and happy life with a great support system of friends, family and colleagues. I know that I am lucky to be alive. I felt I had lady luck, good fortune and God on my side.

By the way, those old heads in the bar were right. I received a Combat Infantry Badge (CIB) and a Purple Heart for injuries sustained during combat.

D/1-506th Curahee Veterans at Kenny Kays grave at Maple Hill Cemetery. (L-r) Roger Crabb, Hoyt Bruce Moore, lll, (A Co, lst Bn 1970-1971), Kenny David, Tony Cox; Greg Phillips, Don Shaughnessy; Merle Delagrange, Steve "Greek" Avgerinos, and John "Ernie" Banks. Kneeling is Randy Mills, author of "Troubled Hero: A Medal of Honor, Vietnam," and the "War at Home." Photo: Purple Heart Magazine November/December 2007

215

L-r: Mike Campbell, Jack Lemmon: both E 2/501st
Monte Foltz, D 2/506th, Don Shaughnessy, D 1/506th

Volunteers at Elks Annual Veterans Dinner

Elks provides free meals to all veterans on
Veterans Day in Ashtabula County

Don Shaughnessy

Member VFW #943 Ashtabula, Ohio-Lifetime Member

Member American Legion #103 Ashtabula, Ohio- 24yrs

Member DAV Ashtabula, Ohio-Lifetime Member

Vietnam History-continued

After we left, the number of troops continued to decline. Although Nixon reduced our involvement in Vietnam, the number of dead rose as the fighting in the field continued. Troop levels dropped to 335,000 in 1970, but more than 6,000 soldiers died. By the end of 1971, only 150,000 troops remained but still nearly 2,400 Americans were killed. As GIs were rotated home, about 560 soldiers died in 1972 when troop levels fell to an average of 70,000 and to 24,000 by year end. Nixon was signaling to the North Vietnamese that he was pulling out, but they continued to pursue an aggressive posture.

Nixon also promised that he would end the draft and he did, replacing it with a lottery. It was assumed that this would placate those against the war, but it was like putting lipstick on a pig. As the war became more unpopular, those drafted by the lottery were even less enthusiastic toward the war. They had spent many years in the U.S. listening to the inescapable public outcry against the war, witnessed the casualties mount and were less inclined to carry out their duties as had their predecessors. The drug use escalated, especially in base camps and the open refusal to participate in fighting became more prevalent. Fragging of officers and NCOs increased.

President Nixon made headlines in February 1972 with his visiting Mao Tse-tung in China and opening up diplomatic relations. He continued to withdraw troops and felt that the end of the war was within his grasp.

The ARVN continued their fighting largely supported by B-52 bombings and the Air Force provided strategic cover for their troops. Helicopters remained a main focus of the war effort both in the insertions and extractions of troops in the field. Negotiations continued and Nixon and Kissinger were optimistic that they would finally achieve their desired goal of "peace with honor."

But, General Giap ordered 200,000 NVA soldiers to strike Quang Tri just north of Hue, Kontum in the Central Highlands and An Loc in the south in April 1972, known as the Easter Offensive.

Nixon was enraged and ordered bombings on a massive scale along the Cambodian border and nearly 150 miles into North Vietnam, including Hanoi and Haiphong. However, the loss of American planes was costly as fifteen B-52 bombers were shot from the sky by Surface to Air Missiles (SAMs). By the fall of 1972, the bombings had a major impact as the NVA advances slowed. General Giap's Easter Offensive had failed and the North lost 40,000 soldiers resulting in Giap losing his command position, the leader of the war movement since the 1950s.

In late 1972, Kissinger thought he had a peace agreement, and announced that "peace is at hand," just prior to the U.S. elections pitting Nixon against George McGovern, a staunch anti-war campaigner. President Thieu rejected any agreement that allowed the North to take over the South by force. The North countered by stating the American POWs would be held until an agreement was reached. However, Nixon won the election in a landslide, winning all but one state.

Kissinger, with the support of the president, answered with another bombing campaign and informed the North that the "Christmas bombings of Hanoi" would continue until an agreement was reached. In the final days of 1972, negotiations restarted. Finally, on January 23, 1973, a cease-fire agreement was reached. Nixon invited South Vietnam's President Thieu to his San Clemente home in California and promised that the U.S. would respond militarily if the North violated the peace treaty. The final peace treaty was signed on January 27, 1973. The Vietnam Conflict ended for the United States.

By this time, the majority of the American troops had been withdrawn except for 16,000 advisers. The U.S. agreed to pull the few remaining troops out of South Vietnam within sixty days. In short, the agreement was virtually all that had been desired by the North Vietnamese since negotiations began in the mid-1960s.

Vice-President Spiro Agnew was convicted of bribery and was replaced by Gerald Ford. In late 1973, Congress cut off spending for Vietnam and halted any bombings. The War Powers Act passed, limiting the president to wage any type of war.

Despite the promises kept by Nixon such as the ending of the draft, the reduction in forces in Vietnam and the opening of diplomatic relations with China, these were overshadowed by the ensuing challenge of Watergate. After Nixon resigned on April 9, 1974 and President Gerald Ford took office, he pardoned Nixon and offered clemency for draft dodgers and deserters.

The ARVN (southern forces) continued fighting in spite of the lack of support for the war by the U.S. Although the South still had plenty of helicopters, airplanes and tanks, spare parts and maintenance was non-existent. Ammunition was limited, providing only a few bullets for each soldier. The Chinook helicopters that carried artillery to firebases now only provided basic supplies and carried out refugees as part of the Paris Peace Treaty.

The Soviet Union provided the tanks to the North forces that won decisive battles as they marched toward Saigon. In March 1975 the North attacked Kontum, Pleiku and Ban Me Thuot. President Thieu ordered the troops to abandon the region and head south. When captured, less than ten percent of the 7,000 ARVN Rangers survived. More than 40,000 of the 60,000 civilians and troops leaving the Central Highlands for the coast didn't survive.

As Saigon was about to fall, the American Ambassador Graham Martin reaffirmed to President Thieu that the only support for the South Vietnamese was the Navy for evacuation, and there were no B-52s to support the war effort. President Thieu went on the radio and blasted the U.S. for not making good on our commitment. He went on for ninety minutes until the C.I.A. ushered him away to exile in Taiwan. In some respects, he was right that we did agree to provide supplies and weapons if they signed the treaty. It is arguable whether the South could have withstood the North advances if they were provided the funding, supplies and munitions promised by Nixon. However, it was very clear that they could not last without our aid.

On April 30, 1975, ten Marines were the last to leave Saigon on a chopper as other fleeing civilians crowded on to the final helicopter to leave South Vietnam. Interim president General Duong Van "Big" Minh witnessed the tanks enter the courtyard of the Presidential Palace and went on radio and ordered the ARVN forces to lay down their arms. Communist forces captured the Presidential Palace in Saigon, thus ending the war.

Those friendly to the South and U.S. were dealt with harshly by the NVA and Viet Cong while advancing through South Vietnam. In the book, *We Are Soldiers Still*, by Lt. General Harold Moore and Joseph Galloway, the "Trail of Tears," reveals that the North forces killed nearly half of the 200,000 Vietnamese civilian refugees and ARVN soldiers fleeing the Central Highlands.

The ARVN soldiers were sent to reeducation camps and faced bans on employment. Others were forced to relocate to remote areas and some were killed. Some lost their homes and businesses and fled the country. Nearly one million escaped and some "boat people" sought freedom through Malaysia, Hong Kong, Indonesia while others successfully reached the U.S.

The Montagnards found some protection in their native habitat in the Central Highlands. Although the war was thought to be the end of battles for years, it wasn't to be. The NVA continued to battle former ARVN soldiers and Montagnard tribes.

Those who proposed the domino theory that losing in Vietnam meant other nations would fall to communism were partially correct. The communist Khmer Rouge and Pol Pot took control of Cambodia in the early 1970s. The Khmer Rouge killed an estimated 1.7 million of their people, and hundreds of thousands of Vietnamese who sought refuge from Vietnam. The bodies were dumped in fields, called "the killing fields." In retaliation, the former NVA, now PAVN, the People's Army of Vietnam, attacked Phnom Penh late in 1978. The Cambodian-Vietnamese War lasted until 1991. Skirmishes continued until the Khmer Rouge gave up fighting in 1996.

Aftermath

The greatest cost was the number of young men and women who lost their lives, and the impact on their grieving families. Those severely injured suffer daily along with family members who support them.

Fittingly, the Vietnam Veterans Memorial opened in 1982 and 58,260 names are etched in stone in the order that they died. This includes eight women and 1300 Missing In Action (MIA). When the wall was erected there were 57,179 names on the wall, including fourteen men who returned alive. A few names are added each year as records are updated of men who died after the war from injuries suffered during the war.

In 1993, the Vietnam Women's Memorial Project dedicated the Vietnam Women's Memorial that honors the eight military women and fifty-six civilian American women who died in the war. To find out more about the Vietnam Memorial Wall, please go to www.VirtualWall.org.

This memorial was in sharp contrast to the treatment of indifference or contempt shown to many returning Vietnam Veterans. A book by Bob Greene, *Homecoming: When the Soldiers Returned from Vietnam,* tells the stories of men who returned to face name calling and spitting while others experienced a smooth transition.

More than 2.6 million served in Vietnam and over 500,000 were in combat. Although there were more than 47,000 combat related deaths, the number killed in action was about 38,500 while another nearly 8,700 died from wounds. Over 10,000 of these deaths were due to friendly fire, but given the nature of the fighting described, it is understandable. Another 10,800 died from noncombat causes, such as vehicular accidents, malaria, drowning, murder and suicide.

Although the number of deaths dropped after Nixon took office in 1969, the total dead from then forward were still more than 15,000, or about 25 percent of the total that died in Vietnam.

Enlisted men, ranging from private E-1 through E-9 were the likeliest to get killed, representing more than 31,000 of the total 38,000 combat deaths and, in total, more than 50,000 of the 58,000 plus that died. The average age of those who died in this group was about 23. However, there were about 11,500 young men less than 20 years old that were killed in action (KIA).

Among the officers that died, first lieutenants lost nearly 1,500 men and more than 1,000 captains were killed while 400 second lieutenants died. Since many officers had more training and were older, the average age among officers who died was higher.

The average age of a soldier serving in Vietnam was nineteen. The average age of those killed was 23 versus 26 in World War II. Part of the reason is that those in World War II served until the war was over, whereas those in Vietnam were rotated through after a tour of twelve months, a holdover from the Korean War.

Pilots, gunners and troops on helicopters suffered in the line of duty. More than 3,000 died and 2,300 were injured. About 1,275 pilots died and the remainder was the crew or riders. It is surprising that more were not killed and injured given that they received hostile fire flying into a Hot LZ, which happened on about ten percent of all their missions.

Sadly, the number of soldiers that are permanently disabled is 75,000, with another 80,000 seriously wounded plus 150,000 were lightly wounded. Although some believed that African Americans died more than others, they represent about 7,200 deaths, or 12.3 percent, roughly equal to but still higher than their percent in the general population.

There were about 2,500 missing in action right after the war, but progress has been made recovering many bodies so their families can provide a proper farewell to their loved ones. After the peace treaty was signed in 1973, 591 prisoners were released from the Hanoi Hilton--83 died in captivity. Our allies also suffered casualties as more than 5,000 died and 12,000 were wounded.

Medevac helicopters flew nearly 500,000 missions and over 900,000 men were airlifted with an elapsed time of less than one hour from being wounded to being treated in a hospital.

This was a life saver as less than one percent of those wounded that survived the first 24 hours died. More than 4,600 helicopters were shot down or taken out of service. Another 6,000 were damaged--not including bullet holes.

The impact of the war was measured in lives, but it was also costly to the U.S. government. The total cost of $155 billion translates to $775 billion today and contributed to the economic crisis of the 1970s, along with the high price of oil.

The book *Dirty Little Secrets of the Vietnam War*, by James F. Dunnigan and Albert Nofi provides a wealth of information on all aspects of the Vietnam War.

There were 21,000 draft evaders and 7,500 went to prison. About 92,000 deserted from service and 83,000 were recovered receiving sentences ranging from minor discipline to five years in prison. By the end of the war, there were nearly 9,000 deserters with whereabouts unknown.

A book by Don Lawson *The United States in the Vietnam War* provides a great overview of the issues of the Vietnam War.

Later, the North Vietnamese realized they made a mistake when they interned successful people including civil servants, officers, and professionals such as doctors, lawyers and teachers and put them in concentration "reeducation" camps rather than have them assist in the recovery in the South. As many as one million migrated from South Vietnam, and many of these educated people wound up in the U.S. The North was seen as another invading country and instead of liberating the people; they were "just the new boss, same as the old boss."

The number of communists killed is estimated at between 750,000 to one million and 1-2 million were wounded.

Other related outcomes from the conflict are the 50,000 "Amerasians," those children of Vietnamese women and American men. They have become outcasts from civilian life and were treated harshly, often ostracizing them to becoming beggars and prostitutes. By 1990, some 40,000 were allowed to emigrate to the U.S., and some found their fathers and others were in foster homes.

In 1994, Washington lifted the embargo against Vietnam and now we wear shirts and shorts made there. Many who served there have gone back to visit and some have met those they fought against and, in some instances, in the same battles.

Most Vietnam veterans assimilated back into society rather nicely. Some have suffered mental instability due to the now recognized PTSD, post traumatic stress depression. The VA has reported an estimated 500,000 of the 2.6 million who served in Vietnam have suffered some form of PTSD, often exhibiting the symptoms ten to fifteen years after returning from Vietnam.

Vietnam Veterans have successfully raised families, started businesses, hold public office and are outstanding citizens. Some will talk about their experiences while others prefer to remain silent about their time in Southeast Asia.

Although the healing continues, let us be mindful of the ravages of war. There are combat soldiers who continue to suffer from their ordeal in Vietnam. They experience pain, both physically and mentally, and they need and deserve our empathy and support.

We must use every diplomatic measure possible before we contemplate entering into a war that requires putting men and women into harm's way. We owe it to those who have fought in past wars and to those who will face an enemy in the future.

It is interesting to note that the outcome for North and South Vietnam would have been the same had the French-Indochina peace treaty been enacted and the elections been held in 1956. If Eisenhower had not intervened, it is arguable that the U.S. could have avoided 58,000 deaths, 150,000 severely wounded and saved billions of dollars while avoiding a recession. Did we learn our lesson from Vietnam? You decide.

Statistics

VFW magazine and web sites provided the following information.

- Longest war in U.S. history -11 years. 1964-1975.
- January 1965 –March 1973 were the war years.
- 27 million men were available during that period.
- 9 million served in the military.
- 2.5 million served in South Vietnam.
- Average age of the 58,249 killed was 23 years old.
- Youngest-16 years old, Oldest 62 years old.
- 2/3 of the men who served in Vietnam were volunteers.*
- 2/3 of the men who served in WW II were drafted.
- Average age of an infantry man in Vietnam was 19.
- The average age of a soldier in WW II was 26.**
- The average infantryman in the South Pacific during WWII saw about 40 days of combat in four years.
- The average infantryman in Vietnam saw about 240 days of combat in one year due to the mobility of the helicopter.
- Deadliest Day in Vietnam Jan 31, 1968 = 246
- Deadliest Week in Vietnam Feb 10-17, 1968 = 543
- Peak U.S. Fatality Month February 1968 = 3,895
- Aug 7, 1964 The Gulf of Tonkin Resolution passed the Senate 88-2. The two no votes were Sen. Wayne Morse (D-Oregon) and Sen. Ernest Gruening (D-Alaska). U.S. House passed it 414-0.
- Total U.S. bomb tonnage dropped during:
  WW II= 2,057,244 tons
  Vietnam= 7,078,032 tons (3 ½ times WW II tonnage)
- Most of the deaths by hostile action were inflicted on the infantry, over 70 percent of the Army's 30,950 or 21,578.
- *Many draftees became volunteers to avoid infantry.
- **WWII draftees remained in the service until the war ended. In Vietnam, GIs served 12-13 month tours.

By Division	Killed in Action
1st Cavalry-	5,444
25th Infantry-	4,547
23rd (Americal) -	4,040
101st Airborne -	4,011
1st Infantry -	3,146
9th Infantry -	2,624
4th Infantry -	2,531
173rd Airborne Brig.	1,748

State	Total Deaths
California	5,575
New York	4,119
Texas	3,416
Pennsylvania	3,146
Ohio	3,094
Illinois	2,932
Michigan	2,655
Florida	1,953
North Carolina	1,612
Georgia	1,581

Year	Troops	Total dead
1956-65	184,300	2,264*
1966	385,300	6,053
1967	485,600	11,058
1968	536,100	16,511
1969	475,200	11,527
1970	334,600	6,081
1971	156,800	2,357
1972	24,200	968
1973-98	250	1,346*
Total		58,165

*Cumulative losses for early and later years combined.

U.S. Deaths by Military Service	
Army	30,950
Marines	13,091
Air Force	1,744
Navy	1,628
Total	47,413
VFW Magazine-June/July 2003	

U.S. War Deaths 1860-1980

	All Deaths	Combat Deaths
Civil War	558,500	184,600
WWI	116,800	53,500
WWII	407,300	292,100
Korean War	55,000	33,600
Vietnam War	58,249	47,400

Vietnam Ashtabula County Casualties

There were twenty-nine (29) men from Ashtabula County who died in Vietnam. We share this list to honor their service.

Jerry L. Alferink
Robert L. Beaver
Ronald D. Brown
Gerald R. Clemson
Stephen E. Crist
Gary L. Dubach
Larry B. Durst
William J. Endress
David L. Gamble
Thomas R. Grant
John H. Halman
David L. Licate
Donald F. McKiethan
Charles E. McMillion
Robert E. Mackey
Kenneth L. Marshand
Gregory F. Mossford
Nicholas A. Pavlakovich
Randolph R. Ramsey
Ronald L. Rickard
Albert L. Shimek
Stanley J. Shuminski
John M. Tallion
Freddie E. Theis
David R. Thomas
James E. Titus
Craig A. Vanaiken
Lawrence L. White
Terry L. Winters

Source: Ashtabula Star Beacon, August 30, 2009
www.virtualwall.org

REFERENCES AND SUGGESTED READING

Angers, Trent. *The Forgotten Hero, The Hugh Thompson Story*, Acadian Publishing, Lafayette, Louisiana, 1999,

Bahnsen, Brig. Gen. John C. with Wess Roberts, *American Warrior, A Combat Memoir of Vietnam*, Citadel Press, Kensington Publishing Corp., 2007.

Dunnigan, James F., Nofi, Albert A. *Dirty Little Secrets of the Vietnam War*, St. Martin Press, 1999

Coffee, Gerald, Captain, U.S. Navy (Ret), *Beyond Survival*, Coffee Enterprises, Inc., 1990

Karnow, Stanley, *Vietnam, A History*, Viking press, 1983, Penguin Books, 1984

Lawrence, Mark Atwood. *The Vietnam War*, Oxford University Press, 2008

Lawson, Don, *The United States in the Vietnam War*, Thomas Y. Crowell, New York, 1981

McNamara, Robert, *Argument Without End*, Perseus Books Group, 1999

Mills, Randy. *Troubled Hero*, Indiana University Press, 601 North Morton Street, Bloomington, IN 47404-37972006

Moore, Lt. General Harold G. & Joseph Galloway, *We Were Soldiers and Young*, Harper Collins Publishing, 1992

Moore, Lt. General Harold G. & Joseph Galloway, *We Are Soldiers Still*, Harper Collins Publishing, 2008

Nolan, Keith M. *Ripcord*, Presidia Press Book, Random House Publishing, 2000.

Steinman, Ron. *The Soldiers' Story*, Barnes & Noble, Inc., 2009

Weiss, Michael and Mitch. *Tiger Force,* Little, Brown and Company, Time Warner Book Group, 1271 Avenue of the Americas, New York, N.Y. 10020, 2006

NCOC Locator, www.ncoc

Vietnam Remembered Today

VIETNAM GLOSSARY

Air assault. Movement of assault troops by helicopter to an LZ to engage enemy troops or control terrain.

Alpha-alpha. A pattern of claymore mines linked by batter powered electric connections that are detonated by a trip wire.

Ameriasian. A person with mixed American and Asian heritage.

Angel. Hovering helicopter that picks up crashed pilots.

AO. Area of Operations or Tactical Area of Operations.

Ao dai. Vietnamese women's garment consisting of a top split at the waist worn over loose fitting silk trousers.

AP. Armored Piercing.

APC. Armored Personnel Carrier used to transport supplies and personnel.

Army Commendation Medal. The seventh highest medal awarded for meritorious achievement.

Article 15. An article of the military code of justice that a commanding officer may use to punish a soldier for minor offenses without a court martial.

Artillery ambush. Firing artillery as a result of trip flares triggered by the enemy.

ARVN. Army of Republic of South Vietnam.

ASHC. An Assault Support Helicopter Company.

Ash and trash. Noncombative flights to take men from the field to base camp, taking hot food out to the field, evacuating soldiers, etc.

A Shau Valley. One of the strategic entry points for the NVA off the Ho Chi Minh trail and center of supplies, communications and troops. Repeated battles over the territory occurred, notably Hamburger Hill in 1969.

A.W.O.L. Absent without leave.

Bandolier. Canvas belts that held ammunition for machine gun magazines for the M16, carried over the shoulder.

Battalion. Consisting of 4-6 companies or 300-1,000 soldiers commanded by a lieutenant colonel and a sergeant major.

B.C.D. Bad conduct discharge.

B.D.A. Bomb damage assessment.

Beans and Dicks. C-ration hot dogs and beans.

Beans and motherfuckers. C-rations lima beans and ham.

B-52. U.S. Air Force heavy duty bomber. Could carry 84 500 pound bombs inside and 24 750 pound bombs under wings.

Beehive. A large shotgun shell used in close battle situations containing several "flechettes" or tiny steel arrows.

Berm. A mound of earth built up to divide rice patties.

Bird. Common name for aircraft, mostly helicopters.

Bird Dog. Forward air controller (FAC) A small maneuverable, singe engines propeller airplane.

Body count. Number of enemy killed.

Boo-coo, or Boo-koo. Means plenty, or lots, or many. From the French word, beaucoup.

Boonies. An area away from a base camp, typically the jungle.

Boonie hat. Soft hat worn by combat infantrymen, or boonie rat.

Boonie rat. Combat infantrymen.

Boot. New, inexperienced soldier just out of boot camp.

Bouncing Betty. A mine or booby trap that pops into the air about three feet prior to detonating.

Bravo. Army term for infantryman.

Break squelch. A way to communicate when talking to not give away their location.

Bring smoke. To deliver massive amounts of artillery and firepower on an enemy location.

Broken Arrow. Serviceman who was unfaithful to his wife or girlfriend.

Bronze Star. The fifth highest award given for heroic or meritorious achievement of service.

Bunker Complex. Structures built by the VC/NVA to store munitions, personnel and supplies as a field base.

Bush. Term used for being in the field or jungle.

Buy the farm. To be killed.

Cs. Canned meals, C-rations.

C.A. Combat assault. Dropping troops into an LZ.

C-4. a lightweight and malleable explosive like play dough that will only explode using a detonation device.

C&C. Command and Control.

CAS. Close Air Support, air power to support ground troops in combat.

Charlie. The enemy soldier, also called Chuck or Chas.

Cherry. A new inexperienced guy in the unit, a.k.a. NFG.

Chicken Plate. Chest armor worn by helicopter gunners and pilots.

Chow. Military food.

Clicker. Hand held firing device for a claymore mine.

Claymore Mine. Anti-personnel mine used as a perimeter defense weapon using over 600 metal balls with a range of 50-100 meters.

Cluster fuck. Where an operation went poorly and ends in disaster.

Cobra. An attack helicopter armed with rockets and machine guns.

Combat Assault. (CA) Same as air assault.

Company. Three to five platoons, about 60-190 soldiers, typically commanded by a captain with a first sergeant as NCO.

Company grade. A commissioned officer holding rank of lieutenant or captain.

Concertina wire. Coiled barbed wire used for defensive and perimeter situations.

CONUS. The forty eight contiguous states of the U.S.

C.P. pills. Anti-malaria pills.

C-rations. Prepackaged canned meals provided mainly to those in remote locations weighing about 2 pounds with five meal options and included toilet paper, tobacco and snacks.

Crunchie. A grunt, or infantryman who crunches through the jungle.

CS. Tear gas used on the enemy, especially used in tunnels.

C.Y.A. Cover your ass.

DEROS. Date Eligible for Return from OverSeas, or the date the tour for a soldier was to end, a very important date.

Det cord. A Detonation Cord to set off demolition charges, and claymore mines.

Deuce-and-a-half. An Army 2.5 ton truck.

Didi (mau). Vietnamese for go away quickly, or get lost.

DMZ. A three to five mile DeMilitarized Zone separating North and South Vietnam established in the 1954 peace accords.

Doc. Medic.

Dope. Marijuana or other drugs.

Dustoff. A helicopter medevac mission. Named in honor of Lt. Paul Kelley after his death in 1964 on a medevac mission as his radio call sign was "dust-off."

E&E. Escape and Evasion from enemy hands.

ECM. Electronic Counter Measures to jam enemy radar and electronics.

EOD. Explosive Ordnance Disposal. Eliminating or getting rid of unexploded explosives, bombs, booby traps, etc.

E-Tool. Entrenching tool or shovel for digging foxholes.

E.T.S. Estimated Time of Separation from service.

Executive Officer. XO. The second person in command.

Extraction. Withdrawal of troops from an area of operations (AO).

FAC. Forward Air Controller who were with combat units or flew light observation aircraft to coordinate air support between ground troops and tactical aircraft.

Fatigues. Standard military uniform, olive green in color.

Fat Albert. Known as a C-5A aircraft for its ability to carry a lot of stuff.

Field grade. A commissioned officer with rank of major, lieutenant colonel or colonel.

Field of fire. Area that a fire base can support the infantry.

Fire fight. Ground battle between infantry, often short in duration.

Fire for effect. Open up fire with all you got.

Firecracker. An artillery round that is blown up high containing small bombs that hit the ground and then explode.

FSB. Fire Support Base. Artillery and infantry support base located from base camps to support ground troops.

Flak Jacket. A vest to protect against enemy fire shrapnel, weighing 8.5 pounds.

Flechette. Small darts, hundreds packed into a round.

FNG. Fucking New Guy, or new guy in Vietnam.

FO. Forward Observer. Usually a field artillery lieutenant or captain who calls in artillery or air support or Navy gunfire.

Frag. A fragmentation grenade.

Fragging. Where a grenade warning was sent into an officer or NCO because of dislike of a policy.

Freedom bird. An airplane that transport troops home after their tour.

Free-fire zone. Where troops could fire at any enemy movement without permission. Occasionally abused resulting in killing civilians.

Friendly fire. When U.S. or allied forces fired on their own troops inadvertently.

GI. Government Issue. Common for military soldier.

Gook. A slang term for a Vietnamese person.

Grunt. Common name for infantryman.

Gun Truck. 2.5 ton truck equipped with a .50 caliber machine guns plus other weapons.

Gunship. Helicopter with armaments to battle the enemy.

Hanoi Hilton. The prison camp in Hanoi (Hoa Loa Prison) where American prisoners were held.

Head. Common term for bathroom.

Heat Tabs. Flammable tablet used to heat C-rations. C-4 was also used.

Hercules. Name for AC-130 aircraft.

Highway One. The road from the North into Saigon along the coast.

Ho Chi Minh Sandals. Sandals made from tires, the bottom from the tread and the top from the inner tubes.

Ho Chi Minh Trail. Jungle routes from the North through Laos and Cambodia to provide troops, food, and ammunition.

Honey-dippers. Name for those who burned human excrement.

Hooch. Name for Vietnamese simple dwelling, also used for government sleeping quarters or tents.

Hoochgirl. Vietnamese girl employed as maid or laundress.

Hot Hoist. Name for extracting a soldier while under fire.

Hot L.Z. Landing zone under enemy fire.

Huey. Name for UH-1 helicopter. Used for inserting and extracting troops in air assault and dust-offs to retrieve wounded soldiers. Without protruding weapons, it was called a Slick.

Hump. To move on foot with a heavy rucksack.

Incoming. Enemy mortar or rocket fire attack.

In country. In Vietnam.

Intel. Intelligence.

In the Field. Outside of base camp, in a combat area.

Ivy Division. Nickname for the 4th Infantry Division as its patch has four ivy leaves.

Jody. A person who takes out your girl friend or spouse while you are overseas.

Jungle fatigues. Lightweight duty uniform designed for tropical areas.

Jump School. Another name for Airborne training.

Khmer Rouge. Cambodian communists.

KIA. Killed In Action.

Kit Carson Scout. Former NVA now supporting the U.S. used for their knowledge of the terrain and enemy.

Klick. A Kilometer, or a thousand meters.

L.A.W. Light anti-tank weapon. Disposable one-shot shoulder fired rocket launcher.

Loach. A Light Observation Helicopter.

LP. Listening Post, located along the perimeter to track enemy activity.

Long Binh. Largest storage facility in South Vietnam with numerous jeeps, trucks and other equipment.

LBJ. Long Binh Jail. Where U.S. service men were sent as prisoners for acts in violation of laws.

Lifers. Career military soldiers.

Lock and Load. Chambering a round in a weapon.

LRRP. Long Range Reconnaissance Patrol. Pronounced Lurps, or a group of 5-7 men who went into the jungle to observe the enemy without initiating contact. Also a term for ration packs now known as MREs.

L.S.A. Small arms lubricant.

LZ. Landing Zone. Where helicopters landed. Sometimes created by a LZ cut, a large bomb dropped from a C-130 to level vegetation and create an LZ.

MACV. Military Assistance Command, Vietnam, the primary command in Vietnam.

M-16. machine gun that replaced the M-14 in 1968 weighing 7.7 lb. with a 22 round magazine, range of 450 meters.

Mad Minute. All out fire at the maximum rate.

Mama San. Older Asian women, also a head of a brothel.

MASH. Mobile Army Surgical Hospital.

Medevac. A medical evacuation of a soldier, normally by helicopter.

Medal of Honor. The highest of seven medals for gallantry in action against an enemy of the U.S.

Mess Hall. Where soldiers ate.

MIA. Missing In Action.

Mike-mike. Term for millimeters.

Million dollar wound. Non-crippling wound, but enough to return to U.S.

MOS. Military Occupation Specialty, of the many hundred of jobs in the military.

MP. Military Police. Responsible for disciplining troops, traffic control, escorting convoys and guards.

MPC. Military Payment Currency. Used in place of dollars.

Nails. Flechette rounds for the 2.75 in. rocket launcher.

Nape. Short for napalm, a jello substance mixed with gasoline that burns and sucks the oxygen from the air.

NCO Club. Non-Commissioned Officers Club, a place to drink and socialize usually reserved for E-5-E-9, with exceptions.

NDP. Night Defensive Position. Perimeter set up at night by combat troops in the field.

Number One. Denotes very good.

Number Ten. Denotes very bad.

Nuoc mam. Fermented fish sauce that smelled horrible.

N.L.F. National Liberation Front, the Vietcong.

NVA. North Vietnamese Army.

O.C.S. Officer Candidate School.

O.D. Olive Drab. A camouflage color of the Army uniform.

Ps. Piastres, or South Vietnam currency, essentially worthless.

P-38. Army can opener.

Papa san. Older Vietnamese man.

PAVN. People's Army North Vietnam, commonly called NVA.

Perimeter. Outer limit of a military position.

PF. Popular forces of South Vietnam that bore much of the fighting.

PCOD. Pussy Cut Off Date. Time when a soldiers should stop having sex before a soldier was to go home.

Piss-tube. Tube buried in the ground for urinating.

Platoon. Led by a lieutenant and NCO as second in command consisting of 2-4 squads or 16-40 soldiers.

Point Man. The lead soldier in an infantry patrol, watching for booby traps, and enemy movement.

Pop. To throw a grenade, flare or smoke grenade.

POW. Prisoner of War.

PRC-25. A radio used by infantrymen weighing 23 lbs.

Property Books. A listing of equipment and material issued to a unit and the commander is accountable.

PRVN. People's Republic of Vietnam, or North Vietnam.

PTSD. Post-Traumatic Stress Disorder, then known as PTS, for emotional problems from stress of combat.

Puff and Puff the Magic Dragon. Fixed wing airships mounted with 7.62 mm guns firing 6,000 rounds a minute.

Punji Stick. Booby trap used by enemy from sharpened bamboo stakes smeared with feces to add toxic poison.

Purple Heart. A medal awarded for a soldier wounded or killed in combat or hostile action against an enemy of the U.S.

PX. Post Exchange, where soldiers buy food, drinks and clothing.

R & R. Rest and Recreation or Recuperation offered to troops after about six months in Vietnam to take a 3-7 day break in a number of countries or in Vietnam, China Beach, being a favorite.

Rangers. Elite commandos and infantry that are highly trained for recon and combat missions.

Recon. Abbreviation for Reconnaissance.

RA. Regular Army. Those who enlisted in the Army vs. draftees.

REMF. Rear Echelon Mother Fucker. A person who supports the combat troops.

Re-up. To reenlist.

RIF. Reduction In Force.

ROK. Republic of Korea and anything related.

Rome Plow. Bulldozer with a large blade to clear jungle and undergrowth. Made in Rome, Ga.

RON. Remain Overnight Position. A one night defensive position set up by combat troops in the field.

Rotate. To return to the U.S. after a tour in Vietnam.

R.O.T.C. Reserve Officers Training Corps. Program offered in high schools and colleges to prepare students for military officers.

Round Eye. Slang for non-Asians, such as Americans or Europeans.

RPG. Rocket Propelled Grenade. Anti tank grenade launcher.

RTO. Radio Telephone Operator who carried the PRC-25 radio into combat, and was a desired target.

Ruck. Abbreviation for rucksack, or backpack to carry supplies, ammo, food, etc.

RVN. Republic of Vietnam, or South Vietnam.

Saddle up. To put on the rucksack and get ready to move.

Same-same. Same as something, same old thing.

Sappers. Special NVA/VC assault troops who carried explosives called satchel charges, and would sneak into base camps to blow up munitions, helicopters and men.

SAR. Search and Rescue for downed pilots.

Satchel Charges. Pack filled with explosives used by VC and NVA.

Search and Destroy. Troops going on patrol with intent to locate and destroy the enemy.

S.E.R.T.S. Screaming Eagles Replacement Training School.

Shake 'n Bake. Term for person who is put through specialized training and they become an NCO or officer in short period of time.

Short timer. Person who has little time left to serve in their tour.

Shotgun. Door gunners on helicopters or truck guards to protect others when on convoys.

Shrapnel. Metal fragments from a bomb, grenade, artillery or mortar round.

Sitrep. Situation Report, typically a verbal report.

Sky pilot. The chaplain.

Slack man. The second man on patrol, behind the point man.

Slick. A helicopter used for transporting troops and supplies, an air assault helicopter to put troops into combat.

Slope. Slang term for an Asian, or slope eyes.

S.N.A.F.U. Situation normal, all fucked up.

Snake. A Cobra helicopter.

SOG. Special Operations Group.

SOP. Standard Operation Procedure. Established procedures for many contingencies.

SPC. Specialist such as a SP4 or SP5, nearly but not quite equivalent to a corporal or sergeant respectively, serving in a technical position.

Spider Hole. Foxhole of VC/NVA to camouflage a soldier.

Stand down. After an operation or drill, soldiers took a break for rest, or reorganization.

Steel Pot. Standard Army helmet.

Sterilize. To leave a campsite in its original shape so as to not let the enemy know they were there.

STOL. Short Takeoff and Landing, typically used by C-123 and C-130 airplanes.

Tet. New Year's in the Vietnamese and Chinese calendar celebrated for three days after the first full moon after January 20.

The World. Outside Vietnam, commonly referring to the U.S.

TOC. Tactical Operations Center. Command center for directing base camp defenses and field strategy.

T.O.& E. Table of Organization and Equipment.

Thumper. The M-79 grenade launcher.

Triage. Order of treating patients based on severity of wound.

Trip Flare. Ground flare triggered to give off a bright shower of light for several minutes. Used on the perimeter at night to provide warning of movement.

Triple Canopy Jungle. Thick jungle with plants growing at ground level, intermediate level such as large bushes and high level, like trees.

Valor Device. A V denotes the award for acts performed during direct combat with the enemy.

Viet Cong. Communist forces fighting South Vietnamese and U.S.

Vietnamization. Plan designed to turn over combat operations to the ARVN so U.S. troops could withdraw.

VC. Viet Cong, or Vietnamese Communists.

Warrant Officers. Technical officers who specialized in personnel, supply, generators, motor pool, etc.

Wasted. Killed.

WIA. Wounded In Action.

Willie Pete. White phosphorous, used as a target marker by aircraft.

World, The. The U.S.A.

X.O. Executive Officer. Second in command.

Yards. Short for Montagnards, people of the Central Highlands.

Zippo. Slang term for a flamethrower or sometimes called Zippo squads, who burned down villages.

Zap List. Term for listing of the enemy dead.

Zulu. Casualty report of Americans.

*INDEX